1•2•3 COLORS

Color Day Activities
For Young Children

WARREN PUBLISHING HOUSE, INC.
P.O. Box 2250, EVERETT, WA 98203

Editor: Elizabeth S. McKinnon
Copy Editor: Claudia G. Reid
Contributing Editor: Sue Foster
Production Manager: Gayle Bittinger
Layout: Paula Inmon
Flannelboard Patterns: Cora Bunn
Cover Design: Larry Countryman

ISBN 0-911019-17-0

Library of Congress Catalog Number 87-051241
Printed in the United States of America
Published by: Warren Publishing House, Inc.
                P.O. Box 2250
                Everett, WA 98203

INTRODUCTION

Every day is Color Day for young children. Color stimulates their imaginations. It intrigues their sense of order. It delights their sense of sight.

Colors are everywhere, making them the perfect beginning teaching tool. There are colors to identify and colors to count, colors to match and colors to sort. In every area of learning, colors can be used easily and effectively to teach basic skills.

1·2·3 Colors contains hundreds of activities based on ideas contributed to the TOTLINE newsletter by teachers across the country. The activities in the first nine chapters are grouped by Color Days and include suggestions for art, learning games, language, science, movement, music and snacks. An additional chapter contains activities that can be used for all Color Days as well as activities that are designed for working with more than one color.

To further brighten your Color Days, you will find a seasonal selection of color stories, songs and rhymes, each accompanied by flannelboard patterns to copy and use for making felt cutouts. And to enrich your story and music times, there is a color-filled mini-musical for your children to enjoy.

We invite you now to look through this wonderful collection of color ideas that have worked so well for other teachers. Then paint your classroom with colors and let them be the rainbow bridge to learning for your children.

Jean Warren

CONTENTS

FUN WITH RED

Quick Starts for Red Day

- Take a walk to collect red autumn leaves.
- Eat strawberries.
- Make red heart caterpillars.
- Provide a red wagon for playtime.
- Snack on red apple slices.
- Make red dot-to-dot hearts or apples.
- Glue red tissue paper pieces on drawings of watermelon slices.
- Drink cranberry juice.
- Paint red tulips, red roses or red carnations.
- Make tomato soup.
- Play the game Red Rover.
- Make wax-resist pictures by brushing red paint over crayon drawings.
- Visit a local fire station to see the red fire engines.
- Paint or dye with beet juice.
- Learn the nursery rhyme "The Queen of Hearts" and make Thumb Pie "tarts" with strawberry jam filling (see recipe on p. 54).
- Fingerpaint with white paint, then add a little red to create pink.

Art

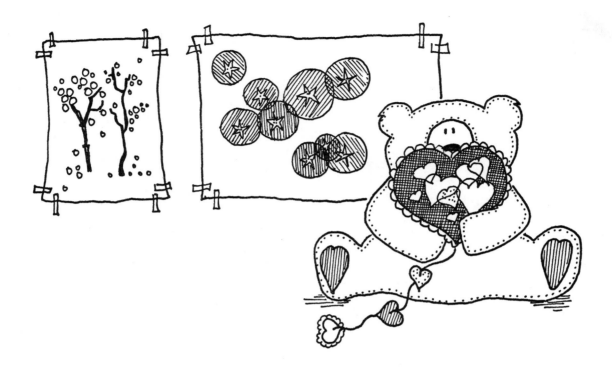

CHERRY TREES

Glue twigs on sheets of white construction paper to make trees. Then let the children attach small red circle sticker "cherries" to their papers, some as if growing on the tree branches and some as if falling off.

Variation: Instead of stickers, use circles punched with a hole punch from red construction paper and let the children glue them on their papers.

APPLE PRINTING

Cut some apples in half vertically and others in half horizontally. (Surprise the children with the hidden "star" that is revealed when an apple is cut horizontally.) Pat the cut surfaces of the apples with a paper towel and allow them to dry for about an hour. Set out sheets of construction paper and pour small amounts of red tempera paint over sponges that have been placed in shallow containers. Then let the children dip the apple halves into the paint and press them on their papers to make prints.

HEART COLLAGES

Set out sheets of white construction paper, small bowls of liquid starch and brushes. Give each child a number of heart shapes cut from red tissue paper. Have the children brush liquid starch on their papers. Then let them place their tissue paper hearts on top of the starch to make collages.

HEART NECKLACES

Let the children help make red playdough by mixing together 1 cup flour, ½ cup salt, 6 to 7 tablespoons water, 1 tablespoon vegetable oil and drops of red food coloring. Have the children roll out the playdough with a rolling pin and use cookie cutters to cut out heart shapes. Place the shapes on sheets of waxed paper and insert a small section cut from a drinking straw in the top of each shape. When the hearts have dried, remove the straw sections and string pieces of red yarn through the holes to make necklaces.

FINGERPAINT APPLES

Cut large apple shapes out of butcher paper and spray on puffs of shaving cream. Then sprinkle on powdered red tempera and let the children fingerpaint on their apple shapes. When the shapes have dried, attach green construction paper leaves to the top of each apple.

RED COLLAGES

Set out sheets of white or red construction paper, scissors and glue. Let the children look through magazines to find red pictures. Then have them cut or tear out the pictures and glue them on their papers to make collages.

Hint: Let younger children choose from precut pictures that have been placed in a box.

VALENTINE COLLAGES

Cut large heart shapes out of red construction paper or tagboard. Then let the children decorate their hearts by gluing on a variety of red items (red lace, red rickrack, red ribbon, red yarn, red heart stickers, red glitter, etc.).

RED LEAF SPATTER PAINTING

Let the children arrange red autumn leaves (or leaves cut from red construction paper) on sheets of white construction paper. Then have them dip toothbrushes in red paint and rub tongue depressors across the toothbrushes to spatter paint on their papers. When the papers have been covered with paint, remove the leaves and let the papers dry. Then mount the paintings on sheets of red construction paper.

Learning Games

HEART HOP

Cut ten large hearts out of red construction paper. Use a black felt-tip marker to number the hearts from 1 to 10, then mix them up. Stand at one end of the room and have the children stand across from you at the other end. As you hold up a heart, have the children hop forward as many hops as the number written on it. Continue holding up the hearts, one at a time, until the children have hopped to your end of the room. Repeat the game by having the children hop back across the room as you hold up the numbered hearts.

Hint: Use age and ability to determine how much help you give with number recognition.

Language

RED WAGON BOOK

Give each child a precut red wagon shape to glue on a sheet of white construction paper. Let the children draw pictures of anything they choose inside their wagons. When they have finished, have them tell you what they drew while you write their responses on the bottoms of their papers. Then staple the papers together with a cover to make your group's very own Red Wagon Book.

COUNTING APPLES

Number ten index cards from 1 to 10. Give each child a paper plate and a plastic sandwich bag containing ten apple shapes cut out of red construction paper. Have the children sit cross-legged on the floor in a circle with their paper plates in front of them. Place a numbered index card on the floor in the center of the circle. Then have the children each count out on their plates the same number of apples as the number on the card. Have them put their apples back into their plastic bags before you place another numbered card in the center of the circle. Continue the game until all the cards have been played.

Variation: Instead of apple shapes, use red paper hearts.

TEN RED APPLES

Ten red apples growing on a tree,
  (Hold hands up high.)
Five for you and five for me.
  (Shake one hand, then the other.)
Help me shake the tree just so,
  (Shake whole body.)
And ten red apples fall down below.
  (Lower hands while fluttering fingers.)
One, two, three, four, five,
  (Count fingers on one hand.)
Six, seven, eight, nine, ten.
  (Count fingers on other hand.)

Author Unknown

Science

Movement

SEND IN THE CLOWNS

Make clown noses by cutting small circles out of red construction paper. Attach the circles to the children's noses with loops of tape rolled sticky side out. Then lead the children in a clown parade, having them imitate clown movements that you make. Let them recite the following poem while they parade around the room:

Red is a stop sign,
Red is a rose.
Red is an apple
And a funny clown's nose!

Sue Foster

Variation: At Christmastime, make red "Rudolph noses" for the children to wear and change the last line of the poem to read: "And Rudolph's shiny nose!"

STOP AND GO

Play a stop-and-go game with a red STOP sign made from construction paper. Choose a movement such as jogging in place or jumping up and down. When you say "Go," have the children start moving. When you hold up the STOP sign, have them stop. Continue the game as long as interest lasts.

RED COLOR SCOPES

Let the children paint toilet tissue tubes red, if desired. When the paint has dried, cover one end of each tube with a 4-inch square of red cellophane and secure it with a rubber band. Then let the children use the tubes like telescopes to view the world around them. Discuss how colors change when they are seen through the red cellophane.

LITTLE RED TRAIN

Have the children sit down and wait in line at an imaginary train station. Chug around the room as everyone recites the poem below. Each time you stop at the station, have the child at the head of the line hook onto your train. Continue until everyone is hooked on and has had a turn chugging around the room.

Little Red Train chugging down the track,
First it goes down, then it comes back.
Hooking on cars as it goes,
Little Red Train just grows and grows.

Jean Warren

12

Music

FOUR RED APPLES
Sung to: "This Old Man"

Four red apples on the tree,
Two for you and two for me.
So-o shake that tree and watch them fall.
One, two, three, four—that is all.

Additional verses: "Four red cherries on the tree; Four red leaves on the tree."

Jean Warren

I'M A BIG RED TOMATO
Sung to: "Little White Duck"

I'm a big red tomato
Growing on the vine,
A big red tomato
Looking oh, so fine.
Now you can make good things with me—
Soup, juice, pizza, to name just three.
I'm a big red tomato
Growing on the vine.
Grow, grow, grow.

Jean Warren

THREE RED VALENTINES
Sung to: "Row, Row, Row Your Boat"

Three red valentines,
Each one with a bow.
Pretty and shiny and lacy, too,
Standing in a row.

Judith E. McNitt
Adrian, MI

Snacks

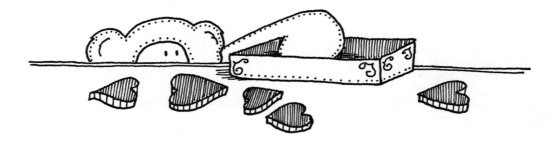

RED GELATIN HEARTS

Thaw ½ cup frozen strawberries and whirl them with the juice in a blender. Stir 4 envelopes unflavored gelatin into 2 cups cold water and heat slowly until gelatin is dissolved. Stir together the strawberries and the gelatin mixture and add 1 6-ounce can unsweetened frozen apple juice concentrate. Spray a 9- by 12-inch pan with non-stick cooking spray. Pour mixture into pan and chill until set. To unmold, turn pan upside down on a countertop. Then cut hearts out of the gelatin with a small heart-shaped cookie cutter. Makes approximately 36 hearts.

TOMATO JUICE

In a blender container, place 1 small can tomatoes, a squeeze of lemon juice, a dash of salt and 3 crushed ice cubes. Whirl ingredients until well blended. Makes 4 servings.

RED PINEAPPLE PUNCH

Mix together 1 large can unsweetened pineapple juice, 6 cups cold water and 1 packet unsweetened Kool-Aid Tropical Punch mix. Stir well and serve over ice in clear plastic cups. Makes 24 small servings.

For additional activities that can be used to teach the color red, see "Fun With Many Colors," beginning on p. 79.

Ideas in this chapter were contributed by:

Valerie Bielsker, Lenexa, KS
Cathy Griffin, Princeton Junction, NJ
Kim Heckert, Adrian, MI
Barb Johnson, Decorah, IA
Elizabeth A. Lokensgard, Appleton, WI
Marian McLean, Sooke, B.C.
Joleen Meier, Marietta, GA
Susan A. Miller, Kutztown, PA

Kathy Monahan, Coon Rapids, MN
Donna Mullennix, Thousand Oaks, CA
Susan Peters, Upland, CA
Dawn Picollelli, Wilmington, DE
Barbara Robinson, Glendale, AZ
Kathy Sizer, Tustin, CA
Gail Weidner, Tustin, CA
Maryann Zucker, Reno, NV

FUN WITH YELLOW

Quick Starts for Yellow Day

- Paint designs with glue and sprinkle on yellow cornmeal.
- Study yellow traffic safety signs.
- Peel bananas and bake them with butter.
- Go on a walk to find spring buttercups or yellow autumn leaves.
- Make deviled eggs or egg salad.
- Play with yellow felt shapes on the flannelboard.
- Make lemonade and taste before and after adding sweetener.
- Paint egg cartons yellow and add black stripes to make bees.
- Serve yellow wax beans at snack time.
- Take a field trip to the local school bus garage and go for a ride on a bright yellow school bus.
- Make chicken noodle soup.
- Use yellow plastic lids for floating toys.
- Fingerpaint on a tabletop with lemon pudding.
- Snack on fresh or canned pineapple.
- Make a group mobile with stars and a moon cut from yellow construction paper.

Art

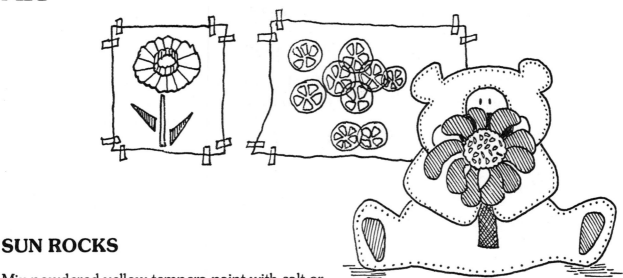

SUN ROCKS

Mix powdered yellow tempera paint with salt or sand and pour it into shaker containers. Give each of the children a rock that has a smooth surface. Have them use Q-Tips to draw suns on their rocks with white glue. Then let them sprinkle the yellow salt or sand over the glue.

SUNFLOWERS

Have the children paint paper plates yellow. While the paint is still wet, let them press yellow crepe paper or tissue paper strips around the edges of their plates to create petals. When the paint has dried, let the children glue sunflower seeds in the centers of their plates. Then attach the finished sunflowers to green construction paper stems and mount them on a wall or a bulletin board.

COTTON BALL CHICKS

Let each child in turn shake two cotton balls in a sack with a mixture of powdered yellow tempera paint and baby powder. Give each of the children a cup cut from a white Styrofoam egg carton. Have them glue their cotton balls inside their egg cups, one on top of the other, to make chicks. Then give them small beaks cut from orange construction paper and eyes cut (or punched with a hole punch) from black construction paper to glue on their chicks' faces.

DAFFODILS

Give each of the children a yellow and a white cupcake liner. Have them flatten one of their liners and spread glue on the center portion. Then have them place their other liners upright on top of the glue to make daffodil flowers. If desired, attach Popsicle sticks or pipe cleaners for stems.

LEMON PRINTING

Cut lemons in half and allow a little time for the cut surfaces to dry. Make paint pads by placing sponges or folded paper towels in shallow containers and pouring on yellow tempera paint. Give each of the children a sheet of white construction paper. Then let them dip the cut surfaces of the lemons into the paint and press them on their papers to make prints.

POPCORN KERNEL NECKLACES

Let the children glue yellow popcorn kernels on 3-inch circles cut from yellow construction paper. When the glue has dried, punch a hole in the top of each circle. Then string pieces of yellow yarn through the holes to make necklaces.

SUNNY SCULPTURES

Have the children dip pieces of yellow yarn into a mixture of white glue and water. Then let them arrange their yarn pieces in designs on sheets of waxed paper. Allow several days for the glue to dry. Then peel off the waxed paper and hang the "sunny sculptures" from the ceiling or in a window.

CORNCOB PRINTING

Wash corncobs and allow them to dry for several days. Make paint pads by placing folded paper towels in shallow containers and pouring on yellow tempera paint. Have the children first roll the corncobs on the paint pads. Then let them roll the cobs across their papers to make prints.

Variation: Use a serrated knife to cut the corncobs in half. Then let the children dip the cutoff ends into the paint and press them on their papers to make yellow corncob "flowers."

DAFFODIL MURAL

On a large sheet of butcher paper, paint or draw a garden of green daffodil stems and leaves. Cut 6-inch flower shapes out of yellow construction paper. Then let the children each glue a yellow cupcake liner in the center of a flower shape to make a daffodil. When they have finished, let the children glue their daffodils on top of the stems on the butcher paper to create a sunny springtime mural.

Learning Games

Language

DAFFY-DOWN-DILLY

Bring in a daffodil and pass it around the group at circle time. Then recite the following nursery rhyme:

Daffy-down-dilly
Has come to town,
In a yellow petticoat
And a green gown.

Explain that "Daffy-down-dilly" is another name for "daffodil." Ask the children to tell which part of the daffodil they think is the yellow petticoat and which part they think is the green gown.

DUCKS IN PONDS

Cut fifteen small duck shapes out of yellow construction paper or tagboard. Use five Styrofoam food trays (blue, if available) for ponds and number them from 1 to 5. Then set out the shapes and the trays and let the children take turns placing the appropriate number of ducks into each pond.

MEASURING WITH CORNMEAL

Pour yellow cornmeal into a plastic dishpan and provide a set of measuring cups. Let the children take turns experimenting with measuring. They will soon discover that it takes four quarter-cups or two half-cups to fill the one-cup container.

BABY CHICKS

Have the children sit in a group. Choose one child to be the Mother Hen and have the child leave the room. Choose two or three other children to be the Baby Chicks and have all the children lower their heads and cover their mouths with their hands. Have the Mother Hen return and walk around the group saying, "Cluck, cluck." As she does so, have the Baby Chicks make peeping sounds. When the Mother Hen thinks that a child is one of her chicks, have her tap the child on the shoulder. If the Mother Hen guesses correctly, have the Baby Chick raise his or her head. When the Mother Hen has found all of her babies, select new players and start the game again.

Science

MAKING BUTTER

Fill baby food jars half full with whipping cream and screw the lids on tightly. Let two children take turns shaking each jar. After about five minutes the cream will be whipped, and after another minute or so, lumps of yellow butter will form. Rinse off the liquid whey and add a little salt, if desired. Then spread the butter on crackers or cornbread for tasting.

DANDELION FUN

Go on a walk with the children to look for dandelions. Let each child pick a small handful, then tie their bouquets with yellow yarn bows. If desired, dig up a dandelion to take back to the room for the children to replant and care for.

Movement

SUNS IN THE SKY

Have the children stand about 3 feet apart and give them each a yellow balloon "sun." Have them bat their balloon suns up into the air and try keeping them up without moving from their spaces. When a balloon falls outside of a child's space or reach, have the child sit down. Continue the game until no one remains standing.

STAR SEARCH

Cut stars out of yellow construction paper and hide them around the room. Give each of the children a paper bag to decorate with a yellow crayon. Then play or sing the song "Twinkle, Twinkle, Little Star" and have the children begin searching for the hidden stars to place in their decorated bags. Let them continue searching as long as they hear the music. Then have them stand still each time the music stops. Continue the game until all the stars have been found.

Variation: Let the children sing this version of "Twinkle, Twinkle, Little Star" while they are searching:

> Twinkle, Twinkle, yellow star,
> How I wonder where you are.
> Let's go looking here and there,
> Let's go looking everywhere.
> Twinkle, twinkle, yellow star,
> How I wonder where you are.

Jean Warren

Music

OVER IN THE BARNYARD
Sung to: "Down by the Station"

Over in the barnyard
Early in the morning,
See the yellow chickies
Standing in a row.
See the busy farmer
Giving them their breakfast.
Cheep, cheep, cheep, cheep.
Off they go.

Repeat, substituting the word "duckies" for "chickies"
and "quack" for "cheep."

Jean Warren

WE'RE LITTLE YELLOW DUCKS
Sung to: "Little White Duck"

We're little yellow ducks
Who love to see the rain,
Little yellow ducks,
Now we will explain.
We love to see the rain come down,
Making puddles all over town.
Oh, we're little yellow ducks
Who love to see the rain.
Splish, splish, splash!

We're little yellow ducks
Who love to swim and splash.
We wish the rain
Would last and last and last.
We love to see the rain come down,
Then we can swim all over town.
Oh, we're little yellow ducks
Who love to see the rain.
Splish, splish, splash!

Jean Warren

BRIGHT SUN
Sung to: "Row, Row, Row Your Boat"

Bright sun shining down,
   (Move hands down slowly, fingers apart.)
Shining on the ground.
What a lovely face you have,
   (Hold arms in circle above head.)
Yellow, big and round.

Susan A. Miller
Kutztown, PA

Snacks

BANANA PUDDING

For each child place 1 tablespoon instant banana pudding mix into a baby food jar. Add 2 tablespoons cold milk and watch as the contents turn yellow. Put lids securely on the jars and have the children shake them for about 45 seconds. Then let the children eat their pudding with small spoons. Serve with sliced bananas, if desired.

PINEAPPLE MILKSHAKES

In a blender container, place 1 cup unsweetened pineapple juice, ¼ cup dry nonfat milk, 1 small sliced banana, 1 teaspoon vanilla and 1 egg (optional). Whirl ingredients until well blended. Makes 4 small servings.

CORNBREAD

In a large bowl, mix together 1 cup flour, 1 cup yellow cornmeal, ½ teaspoon salt and 1 tablespoon baking powder. In a blender container, place ½ cup unsweetened frozen apple juice concentrate, 1 egg, ½ cup milk, ¼ cup vegetable oil and 1 sliced banana. Blend well and stir mixture into dry ingredients. Pour batter into a greased 9-inch baking pan and bake at 400 degrees for 25 to 30 minutes. Makes 16 small squares.

For additional activities that can be used to teach the color yellow, see "Fun With Many Colors," beginning on p. 79.

Ideas in this chapter were contributed by:

Valerie Bielsker, Lenexa, KS
Tamara Clohessy, Weaverville, CA
Marjorie Debowy, Stony Brook, NY
Cindy Dingwall, Palatine, IL
Lisa Fransen, Tucson, AZ
Cathy Griffin, Princeton Junction, NJ
Barb Johnson, Decorah, IA
Elizabeth A. Lokensgard, Appleton, WI

Judith E. McNitt, Adrian, MI
Susan A. Miller, Kutztown, PA
Kathy Monahan, Coon Rapids, MN
Susan Peters, Upland, CA
Nancy Ridgeway, Bradford, PA
Bonnie Rogers, Olympia, WA
Saundra Winnett, Fort Worth, TX

FUN WITH BLUE

Quick Starts for Blue Day

- Paint pictures of the blue sky.
- Spread blue icing on cookies to create "cookie monsters."
- Count how many in the group have blue eyes.
- Touch and examine bluebells, morning glories and blue daisies.
- Read *Blueberries for Sal* by Robert McClosky.
- Use blue aquarium gravel for sandbox play.
- Go on a field trip to pick and eat blueberries.
- Cut and fold blue origami paper.
- Take a walk to mail letters in a blue mailbox.
- Add blue food coloring to milk at snack time.
- Fingerpaint blue ocean waves.
- Snack on blueberry yogurt.
- Learn the nursery rhyme "Little Boy Blue" (see p. 29).
- Make blueberry pancakes.
- Glue pants shapes cut from old blue jeans on drawings of clotheslines.
- Talk about plants and animals that live in the blue sea.

Art

BLUE BUBBLE PRINTS

In a small margarine tub, mix one part blue liquid tempera paint with two parts liquid dishwashing detergent and stir in a small amount of water. Let one child at a time put a straw into the paint mixture and blow through it until the bubbles rise above the rim of the margarine tub. Then lay a piece of white paper on top of the bubbles and let the child rub across it gently. As the bubbles break, they will leave delicate blue prints on the paper.

Hint: To prevent the children from accidentally sucking up the paint mixture, poke holes near the tops of the straws.

COOKIE CUTTER PRINTS

Mix tempera paints to make various shades of blue. Start by adding blue to white paint, making each shade darker than the one before it. To darken blue, begin with blue paint and add small amounts of black. Pour the paints into shallow containers and set out sheets of white construction paper and various kinds of cookie cutters. Then let the children dip the cookie cutters into the paint and press them on their papers to make prints. When the paint has dried, mount the prints on sheets of blue construction paper.

BLUE MURAL

Attach a large sheet of butcher paper to a wall. Let the children look through magazines and tear out pictures of blue items. Then have them brush thick blue paint on the butcher paper and press the magazine pictures on the wet paint to create a blue mural.

MARBLE PAINTING

For each child place a circle cut from white construction paper in the bottom of an aluminum pie tin and put several spoonfuls of blue tempera paint in the center. Then give the child one or two marbles to roll back and forth over the paint until the paper is crisscrossed with blue designs.

FORGET-ME-NOTS

Draw leafy forget-me-not stems on sheets of white construction paper. Let the children glue small pieces torn from blue facial tissue all over their stems to make blossoms. Then let them use a hole punch to punch circles out of white construction paper and glue them in the centers of their blossoms. While doing this activity, talk about how forget-me-nots are considered to be flowers of friendship.

BLUEBERRY PIES

Cut small pie shapes out of tan construction paper. Let the children use a hole punch to punch circles out of dark blue construction paper. Then have them brush glue on their pie shapes and cover the glue with blue circle "blueberries."

Variation: Instead of circles punched out of construction paper, use small blue circle stickers.

BLUEBELLS

Cut egg cups out of cardboard egg cartons. Then cut the cups into bluebell shapes and let the children paint them light blue. When the paint has dried, make stems by inserting the ends of green pipe cleaners through the bottoms of the bluebells, then bending the pipe cleaners into cane shapes. If desired, let the children poke holes in the ends of precut green construction paper leaves and thread them on their bluebell stems.

BLUE WEAVINGS

Cut slits around the edges of Styrofoam food trays (use blue trays, if available). Cut blue yarn into manageable lengths and tape one piece to the back of each tray. Then let the children wind the yarn around their trays, each time passing it through one of the slits. Encourage them to crisscross their trays in any way they wish to create designs. When the children have finished, trim the ends of the yarn and tape them to the backs of the trays. Attach loops of yarn for hangers, if desired.

BLUE DAY HATS

Use newspaper or construction paper to make a hat for each child. Set out glue and materials such as the following: blue yarn, blue cupcake liners, blue buttons, blue glitter, blue paper scraps, blue sequins, blue felt-tip markers, blue crayons, blue chalk. Then let the children use the materials to decorate their hats any way they wish.

Learning Games

BLUEBERRY MATCHING GAME

Cut twelve bush shapes out of green construction paper and glue each shape on an index card. Divide the cards into six pairs. Then number the pairs of cards from 1 to 6 by attaching the appropriate number of small blue circle stickers to the bush shapes (or by gluing on circles cut or punched out of blue construction paper). Then mix up the cards and let the children sort them into pairs by matching the numbers of "blueberries" on the bushes.

Science

FISH TANK

Fill a large plastic soft drink bottle about one quarter full with water. Add a few drops of blue food coloring and a drop of liquid detergent. Pour in a small amount of clean sand or aquarium gravel. Blow up two small balloons, release most of the air, then tie the ends closed. Push the balloons into the bottle and screw the cap on tightly. When you have finished, you will have a fish tank with two bobbing "fish" inside. Let the children take turns holding the bottle sideways and rocking it back and forth to watch the fish "swim" in the blue water.

BLUE CARNATION

Place a white carnation in a glass of water to which you have added a generous amount of blue food coloring. Over the next few days, have the children observe as the petals begin to turn light blue. Use the experiment to discuss how plants take water up through their stems and out into their leaves and flowers.

Language

BLUE MYSTERY BOX

Cover a box with blue construction paper. Just before circle time, hide a blue object (a blue hat, a blue button, a blue crayon, etc.) inside the box. Begin by saying, "There is something inside this box that is blue. What do you think it might be?" Continue to give identifying clues until the children guess what the object is. Repeat the activity for several days, using a different blue item each day.

Hint: For added fun, use a furry blue puppet (named Mr. Blue) to introduce the mystery box and give the clues.

Movement

BLUE SHAPE WALK

Cut at least one large shape for each child out of blue construction paper and several more shapes out of white construction paper. Mix up the shapes and tape them to the floor in a circle. Then play music and let the children walk, skip, hop, gallop, etc., around the shape circle. When you stop the music, have each child find a blue shape to stand on. Continue the game as long as interest lasts.

Music

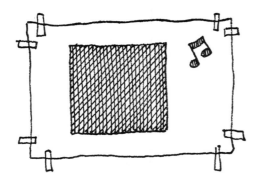

ONE BLUE SQUARE
Sung to: "Three Blind Mice"

One blue square, one blue square,
See how it's shaped, see how it's shaped.
Four big corners it does have,
Four big corners it does have.
One blue square, one blue square.

Hold up a large square of blue construction paper while singing the song.

Mary Kelleher
Lynn, MA

LITTLE BOY BLUE
Sung to: "Twinkle, Twinkle, Little Star"

Little Boy Blue, come blow your horn,
  (Pretend to blow horn.)
The sheep's in the meadow, the cow's in the corn.
  (Point to the right, then to the left.)
Where's the boy who looks after the sheep?
  (Cup hand over eye and look around.)
He's under the haystack, fast asleep.
  (Pretend to sleep.)
Little Boy Blue, come blow your horn,
  (Pretend to blow horn.)
The sheep's in the meadow, the cow's in the corn.
  (Point to the right, then to the left.)

Adapted Traditional

THE BLUEBERRY BUSH
Sung to: "The Mulberry Bush"

Here we go round the blueberry bush,
The blueberry bush, the blueberry bush.
Here we go round the blueberry bush,
So early in the morning.

Pick the blueberries small and round,
Small and round, small and round.
Pick the blueberries small and round,
So early in the morning.

Additional verses: "Taste the blueberries ripe and sweet;
Now let's make some blueberry (pies/jam/muffins/etc.)."

Elizabeth McKinnon

Snacks

BLUEBERRY MUFFINS

In a large bowl, sift together 1 cup white flour, 1 tablespoon baking powder and ½ teaspoon salt. Stir in ¾ cup whole-wheat or graham flour. In a blender, combine 1 egg, ½ cup unsweetened frozen apple juice concentrate, ¼ cup vegetable oil, ½ cup milk and 1 sliced banana. Pour liquid ingredients into dry ingredients and mix well. Stir in 1 cup fresh or canned blueberries. Spoon batter into a well-greased 12-cup muffin tin and bake at 400 degrees for 20 to 25 minutes. Makes 12 servings.

BLUEBERRY SYRUP

In a blender container, place 1 cup blueberries and ½ cup unsweetened frozen apple juice concentrate. Blend well and pour mixture into a saucepan. Bring to a boil over medium heat. Add 1 teaspoon cornstarch that has been mixed with 2 teaspoons water. Boil for 2 minutes, stirring constantly. Remove from heat and stir in ½ teaspoon vanilla. Cool slightly and use as a topping for pancakes or French toast.

For additional activities that can be used to teach the color blue, see "Fun With Many Colors," beginning on p. 79.

Ideas in this chapter were contributed by:

Marian Berry, Tacoma, WA
Valerie Bielsker, Lenexa, KS
Cindy Dingwall, Palatine, IL
Connie Gillilan, Hardy, NE
Peggy Hanley, St. Joseph, MI
Kim Heckert, Adrian, MI
Elizabeth A. Lokensgard, Appleton, WI

Judith E. McNitt, Adrian, MI
Susan A. Miller, Kutztown, PA
Inge Mix, Massapequa, NY
Kathy Monahan, Coon Rapids, MN
Susan Peters, Upland, CA
Nancy Ridgeway, Bradford, PA
Gail Weidner, Tustin, CA

FUN WITH GREEN

Quick Starts for Green Day

- Make leaf rubbings with green crayons.

- Snack on green grapes.

- Take a walk to look for four-leaf clovers.

- Read *Green Eggs and Ham* by Dr. Seuss and eat scrambled eggs tinted with green food coloring.

- Make prints with green vegetables and green paint.

- Sit in the green grass and look carefully for a special "visitor"—an insect, a leaf, a worm, etc.

- Begin a unit on dinosaurs.

- Use frozen green peas for finger snacks.

- Purchase a green shamrock plant to grow in the room.

- Read *Little Blue and Little Yellow* by Leo Lionni.

- Serve green Irish soda bread or green bagels for a special snack.

- Outline shamrock shapes with green macaroni.

- Snack on slices of honeydew melon.

- Plant grass seeds in green plastic pots.

- Glue dried split peas on green paper plates.

- Make an all-green salad using ingredients such as lettuce, spinach, chives, sprouts, cucumbers, zucchini and green peppers.

Art

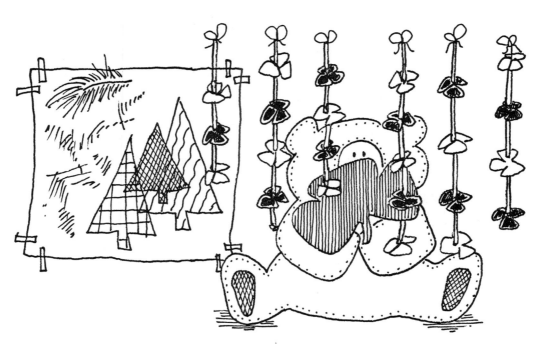

PAINTING WITH EVERGREENS

Cut 3- to 4-inch branch tips from various kinds of evergreens. Set out white construction paper and pour green tempera paint into shallow containers. Then let the children dip the branch tips into the paint and brush them across their papers to create designs. When they have finished, staple each child's branch tip on his or her painting. While doing this activity, discuss the color, smell and texture of the different evergreens.

Variation: Let the children use the branch tips to brush green paint on green construction paper. When the paint has dried, cut each child's paper into an evergreen tree shape. If desired, use the trees to make backgrounds for bulletin board displays.

GREEN PINECONE TREES

Provide each child with a large pinecone. Pour green tempera paint into shallow containers and set out small sponges. Then have the children use the sponges to brush green paint on their pinecones. While the paint is still wet, let them sprinkle on green glitter.

Variation: Instead of glitter, use salt mixed with powdered green tempera paint.

GREEN FORESTS

Cut different sized triangles out of various kinds and shades of green paper (green construction paper, green tissue paper, green crepe paper, green foil wrapping paper, etc.). Then let the children glue the triangle "trees" on sheets of white construction paper to create forests.

LEPRECHAUN LADDERS

Cut white or clear plastic drinking straws into 1½-inch sections. Cut 4-inch shamrock shapes out of green construction paper and punch holes in the centers (make sure that the holes are smaller than the ends of the straw sections). Give each child six shamrock shapes, five straw sections, and a 14-inch length of green yarn with a straw section tied at one end and the other end taped to make a "needle." Then let the children string their shamrock shapes on their pieces of yarn with a straw section between each shamrock. When they have finished, hang their "leprechaun ladders" from the ceiling or in a window.

Hint: For a fun surprise, sprinkle a light dusting of flour on the shamrocks for the children to discover on St. Patrick's Day morning. Explain that the "magic dust" was left by the leprechauns as they climbed and danced on their ladders!

GREEN RICE DECORATIONS

Let the children make green rice shamrocks for St. Patrick's Day or green rice trees for Christmas. Soak rice in a small amount of water mixed with green food coloring. When the desired shade of green has been reached, drain off the water and let the rice dry on paper towels or in pie tins overnight. Cut shamrock shapes or Christmas tree shapes out of green tagboard. Then let the children brush diluted glue on their shapes and sprinkle green rice over the glue.

Variation: Color the rice by shaking it in a clear plastic bag with several drops of green food coloring and several drops of rubbing alcohol. Spread the rice out on paper towels to dry.

GREEN BERRY BASKET PRINTS

Set out green plastic berry baskets and sheets of white construction paper. Pour green tempera paint into shallow containers. Then let the children dip the bottoms of the berry baskets into the paint and press them on their papers to make prints.

HANDPRINT ALLIGATORS

Brush the palm of each child's hand with green tempera paint. Then have the child press his or her hand (with fingers together and thumb extended) on a sheet of black construction paper to make an open-jawed "alligator head." Let the child use brushes to paint the alligator's body, tail and legs with green paint and its sharp teeth with white paint. Then let the child dip the end of a cork into pink paint and use it to print an eye near the top of the alligator's head.

GREEN MONSTERS

Set out sheets of white construction paper, green tempera paint and brushes. Let the children use the brushes to gently spatter green paint on one half of their papers. While the paint is still wet, have them fold their papers and rub across them with their hands. Then let them unfold their papers to discover the "green monsters" they have created.

Variation: Use yellow and blue paint instead of green.

PAINTING WITH FOOD COLORING

Mix yellow food coloring with water in one small clear bowl and blue food coloring with water in another. Demonstrate that blue and yellow make green by pouring one-third of the yellow water and one-third of the blue water into a third bowl. Then let the children use Q-Tips to paint designs on white construction paper with all three colors.

CELLOPHANE COLLAGES

Let the children arrange shapes cut from blue and yellow cellophane between sheets of waxed paper. Encourage them to overlap the edges of the shapes to create green. With an iron set on medium, press each set of waxed paper sheets until they fuse together (cover the waxed paper with newspaper first to prevent sticking). Then tape green construction paper borders around the collages and hang them in a window.

Caution: Activities that involve using an electric iron require adult supervision at all times.

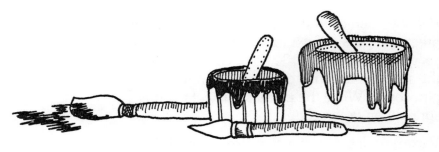

Language

LEPRECHAUN, LEPRECHAUN

Let the children supply the names of green things as you recite the following rhyme:

Leprechaun, Leprechaun,
Come hunt with me.
How many green things can we see?
We found a green (leaf/etc.) under a tree.
We found a green (frog/etc.) next to me.
We found a green (apple/etc.) on the ground.
We found green (caterpillars/etc.) all around.

Jean Warren

Movement

LITTLE GREEN FROGS

Have the children pretend to be little green frogs crouched down in the grass. Then say the rhyme below and have them take big "frog hops" every time they hear the word "hop." When they hear the word "stop," have them stay crouched down without moving.

Little Green Frog, won't you
Hop—hop—hop?
Little Green Frog, won't you
Hop—hop—stop?

Keep repeating the rhyme, each time changing a different "hop" to "stop" so that the children have to listen carefully. Continue the game as long as interest lasts.

Learning Games

SHAMROCK NUMBER MATCHING

For each child write the numerals 1 to 6 in random order on a sheet of light green construction paper. Give the children each six shamrock stickers that have been numbered from 1 to 6. Then let them attach the stickers next to the corresponding numerals on their papers.

Science

GREEN WATER TABLE FUN

Fill your water table tub with water. Squeeze drops of blue and yellow food coloring into the tub and let the children observe as the water turns green. Then add some green floating and sinking toys for the children to play with.

SPROUTING SHAMROCKS

Give each of the children a shamrock shape cut out of terrycloth. Have them place their shamrocks in aluminum pie tins and add a little water. Then let them sprinkle alfalfa seeds all over their shapes. Place the pie tins in a sunny spot and add water regularly. Then let the children observe over the next week as the seeds sprout and turn their shamrocks green.

SCENTED HERB BOOKS

For each child make a four-page book out of white construction paper. Set out small containers filled with dried green herbs such as parsley, sage, oregano, thyme and bay leaves. Discuss the color, smell and texture of the different herbs. Then let the children brush glue on their book pages and sprinkle pinches of herbs on top of the glue.

Hint: To prepare for this activity, ask parents to donate any old herbs they have stored away in the backs of their kitchen cupboards.

Music

ON ST. PATRICK'S DAY
Sung to: "The Mulberry Bush"

Let's wear green and dance a jig,
Dance a jig, dance a jig.
Let's wear green and dance a jig
On St. Patrick's Day.

All join hands and circle round,
Circle round, circle round.
All join hands and circle round
On St. Patrick's Day.

Twirl your partner round about,
Round about, round about.
Twirl your partner round about
On St. Patrick's Day.

Jean Warren

I'M A LITTLE LEPRECHAUN
Sung to: "I'm a Little Teapot"

I'm a little leprechaun
Dressed in green,
The tiniest man
That you ever have seen.
If you ever catch me, so it's told,
I'll give you my pot of gold!

**Vicki Claybrook
Kennewick, WA**

TWO GREEN APPLES
Sung to: "This Old Man"

Way up high in a tree,
(Raise arms high.)
Two green apples smiled at me.
(Smile.)
So I shook that tree as har-r-d as I could.
(Pretend to shake tree.)
Down came the apples. Ummm, they were good!
(Rub stomach.)

Adapted Traditional

DID YOU EVER SEE A LIZARD?
Sung to: "Did You Ever See a Lassie?"

Did you ever see a lizard,
A lizard, a lizard,
Did you ever see a lizard
All dressed up in green?
With green eyes and green nose
And green legs and green toes.
Did you ever see a lizard
All dressed up in green?

**Kim Heckert
Adrian, MI**

37

Snacks

SHAMROCK SANDWICHES

Let the children help make open-faced sandwiches by spreading soft cream cheese on slices of whole-wheat bread. Let each child in turn place an open shamrock-shaped cookie cutter on top of his or her sandwich and fill it with alfalfa sprouts. Then have the child remove the cookie cutter to reveal a green sprout shamrock on top of the cheese.

PUDDING SURPRISE

Spoon ready-made vanilla pudding into small cups and add one drop of blue food coloring and one drop of yellow to each cup. Let the children stir their pudding with spoons and observe what happens. Then let them eat and enjoy their green "pudding surprise" snacks.

GREEN GELATIN SHAMROCKS

Prepare one package of lime gelatin and pour the mixture into a 12-cup muffin tin (fill each cup about half full). Chill until set. To unmold, place the bottom of the pan in a few inches of hot water for about 15 seconds. Then turn the pan upside down on a sheet of waxed paper. Put a lettuce leaf on each plate and carefully place a green gelatin round on top of it. Then use a knife to cut three small triangular notches out of the edge of the round to create a shamrock shape. Add a small piece of celery for a stem and garnish with mayonnaise, if desired. Makes 12 servings.

For additional activities that can be used to teach the color green, see "Fun With Many Colors," beginning on p. 79.

Ideas in this chapter were contributed by:

Valerie Bielsker, Lenexa, KS
Tamara Clohessy, Weaverville, CA
Shirley Crouse, Beverly, KY
Cindy Dingwall, Palatine, IL
Lisa Fransen, Tucson, AZ
Cathy Griffin, Princeton Junction, NJ
Mary Haynes, Lansing, MI
Kim Heckert, Adrian, MI
Sally J. Horton, Waukegan, IL
Julie Israel, Bloomington, IL

Barbara H. Jackson, Denton, TX
Ellen Javernick, Loveland, CO
Barb Johnson, Decorah, IA
Nancy McAndrew, Shavertown, PA
Susan A. Miller, Kutztown, PA
Inge Mix, Massapequa, NY
Susan Peters, Upland, CA
Jane Roake, Oswego, IL
Karen Seehusen, Fort Dodge, IA
Gail Weidner, Tustin, CA

FUN WITH ORANGE

Quick Starts for Orange Day

- Make prints with orange halves and orange paint.
- Snack on carrot sticks.
- Visit a supermarket near Halloween to see the pumpkins on display.
- Squeeze fresh oranges to make orange juice.
- Print with jar lids dipped in different shades of orange paint.
- Purchase an orange marigold plant to care for in the room.
- Make macaroni and cheese.
- Paint paper plates orange and glue on pumpkin seeds.
- Taste orange marmalade.
- Fingerpaint with red and yellow paint.
- Spread orange cheese on round crackers and decorate them with raisin faces.
- Bring in a goldfish for the science table.
- Peel tangerines and divide the sections to share evenly with the group.
- Use orange balloons for water play.
- Carve a pumpkin into a jack-o'-lantern and place a small flashlight inside.
- Snack on dried apricots.

Art

GOLDFISH

Cut large goldfish shapes out of orange construction paper. Pour glue into containers and set out brushes and precut orange tissue paper squares. Have the children brush glue on their fish shapes. Then let them place the tissue paper squares on top of the glue to create scales. When the glue has dried, let the children add eyes and mouths with black felt-tip markers, if desired.

CARROT PRINTING

Cut carrots into sections and carve some of the cutoff ends into shapes such as squares or triangles. Make paint pads by placing folded paper towels in shallow containers and pouring on orange tempera paint. Then let the children dip the carrot sections into the paint and press them on sheets of white construction paper to make prints.

Variation: Print with white paint on orange construction paper.

PUMPKIN PIES

Cut pie shapes out of orange construction paper. Set out small containers of powdered cinnamon and ginger and place a few whole cloves in a paper cup for each child. Have the children brush glue on their pie shapes. Then let them sprinkle the spices over the glue to create fragrant "pumpkin pies."

PLAYDOUGH JACK-O'-LANTERNS

Let the children squeeze lumps of red and yellow playdough together to make orange. Have them press their playdough into plastic lids. Then let them press yellow popcorn kernels into the playdough to create jack-o'-lantern faces. When the playdough has dried, have the children remove their jack-o'-lanterns from the plastic lids, if desired.

PASTA PUMPKINS

Cut pumpkin shapes out of tagboard or lightweight cardboard. Pour glue into small containers and set out bowls of assorted pasta shapes (macaroni, wheels, bows, etc.). Let the children use Popsicle stick applicators to glue the pasta shapes all over their pumpkins. Then after the glue has dried, let them paint their pasta pumpkins orange. If desired, punch holes in the tops of the shapes and insert yarn to make hangers.

Variation: For a glossy effect, use commercial spray paint to paint the shapes orange. (Do spray painting in an area away from the children.)

PAPER BAG PUMPKINS

Have the children fill brown paper lunch bags with scraps of torn newspaper. Secure each bag with a twist tie, leaving about 1 inch gathered at the top. Then let the children paint the bottom parts of their bags orange and the top parts green to create pumpkins with stems. When the paint has dried, string the pumpkins together with green yarn, if desired.

ORANGE LOLLIPOPS

Make a "lollipop" for each child by stapling two small paper plates together (with front sides facing) and attaching a Popsicle stick handle. Then let the children paint their lollipops orange.

Variation: Let the children draw jack-o'-lantern faces on their orange lollipops and use them as puppets for dramatic play.

BLOW PAINT PICTURES

Give each child a piece of white construction paper and a straw. Dribble small amounts of watery red and yellow tempera paint on each paper. Then let the children use their straws to blow the paint across their papers in designs. As the colors mix, they will turn to orange. When the paint has dried, mount the pictures on sheets of orange construction paper.

PUMPKIN PATCHES

Cut small pumpkin shapes out of orange construction paper. Give each child a sheet of white construction paper and a piece of green yarn. Have the children brush glue on their papers and arrange their yarn pieces on top of the glue to make vines. Then let them glue the pumpkin shapes on their vines to create "pumpkin patches."

Learning Games

PUMPKIN SEQUENCING GAME

Cut five or six pumpkin shapes out of orange construction paper, making each one bigger than the one before it. Then mix up the shapes and let the children take turns arranging them in a line from smallest to largest.

Variation: Use orange carrot shapes instead of pumpkin shapes.

PUMPKIN MATCHING GAME

Cut twelve pumpkin shapes out of orange construction paper and glue each shape on a large index card. Draw a different set of facial features on each pair of pumpkins. Then mix up the cards and let the children take turns finding the matching pairs of pumpkin faces.

PUMPKIN FACES

Cut two or three large pumpkin shapes out of orange felt. Use black felt to make six or more different noses, mouths and sets of eyes. Place the felt pumpkins on a tabletop or on the floor. Then let the children take turns arranging the facial features on the pumpkins to create different pumpkin faces.

Variation: Turn this activity into a matching game by drawing different pumpkin faces on index cards and having the children create matching faces on the felt pumpkins.

Science

COLOR MIXING EXPERIMENT

Place three clear plastic glasses filled with water on the science table. Let the children take turns dipping strips of red crepe paper into one glass and strips of yellow into another. When the water in the glasses has turned to red and yellow, let the children dip strips of both colors into the third glass and observe the new color they have created.

ORANGE LEMONADE

Add red food coloring to water in a clear glass or plastic pitcher. Then pour the water into ice cube trays and freeze. When the ice cubes are partially frozen, make lemonade with the children. Give each child a glass of lemonade, a red ice cube to put in it and a Popsicle stick or a small spoon. As the children stir their lemonade, discuss what happens to the color and why it is happening.

Language

ORANGE SURPRISE

Let the children experiment with mixing red and yellow paint while reciting the following poem:

> I took a blob of red paint,
> Then I took a blob of yellow.
> I squished and swished them all around
> As far as they would go.
> My red and yellow began to change,
> And much to my surprise,
> I saw those colors turn to orange,
> Right before my eyes!

Cindy Dingwall
Palatine, IL

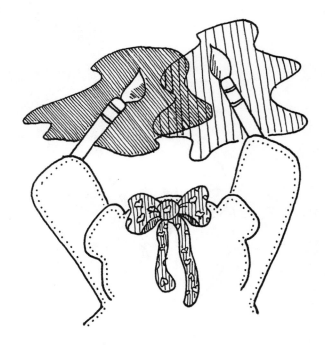

Music

I'M A LITTLE PUMPKIN
Sung to: "I'm a Little Teapot"

I'm a little pumpkin,
Orange and round.
   (Hold arms in circle above head.)
When I'm sad,
My face wears a frown.
   (Frown.)
But when I am happy, all aglow,
Watch my smile just grow and grow!
   (Smile.)

Barbara Hasson
Portland, OR

IF YOU SEE SOMETHING ORANGE
Sung to: "If You're Happy and You Know It"

If you see an orange pumpkin, touch it now.
If you see an orange pumpkin, touch it now.
If you see an orange pumpkin,
If you see an orange pumpkin,
If you see an orange pumpkin, touch it now.

Additional verses: "If you see an orange (crayon/etc.), bring it here; If you see an orange (painting/etc.), point to it." Let the children take turns responding to the directions as you sing each verse of the song.

Marjorie Debowy
Stony Brook, NY

Movement

PUMPKIN PARADE

Hook together three or four cardboard boxes with thick orange yarn and attach a pull cord. Let the children help decorate the sides of the boxes by taping or gluing on large orange construction paper pumpkins. Then play music and let the children take turns pulling their favorite stuffed animals around the room in a "pumpkin parade."

Snacks

JACK-O'-LANTERN SANDWICHES

Let the children help grate cheddar cheese and sprinkle it on top of toasted English muffin halves. Then let them place sliced black olives on top of the cheese to create jack-o'-lantern faces. Place the muffin halves under the broiler for a few minutes before serving.

ORANGE BREW

Use a blender to combine 1 cup milk, 1 6-ounce can unsweetened frozen orange juice concentrate, 1 teaspoon vanilla, 1 egg and 10 to 12 ice cubes. Whirl until thick and frothy, then pour into small cups. Makes 6 to 8 servings.

ORANGE SHERBERT

In a blender container, place 1 12-ounce can unsweetened frozen orange juice concentrate, ¼ cup unsweetened frozen apple juice concentrate, 1 cup dry nonfat milk and 3½ cups water. Blend well. Then pour mixture into a baking pan and place in freezer. Stir thoroughly every hour for 6 to 7 hours. Makes 16 to 20 small servings.

For additional activities that can be used to teach the color orange, see "Fun With Many Colors," beginning on p. 79.

Ideas in this chapter were contributed by:

Valerie Bielsker, Lenexa, KS
Cindy Dingwall, Palatine, IL
Barbara Fletcher, El Cajon, CA
Cathy Griffin, Princeton Junction, NJ
Peggy Hanley, St. Joseph, MI
Barb Johnson, Decorah, IA
Elizabeth A. Lokensgard, Appleton, WI
Alice Marks, Roseville, MN

Judith E. McNitt, Adrian, MI
Susan A. Miller, Kutztown, PA
Kathy Monahan, Coon Rapids, MN
Susan Peters, Upland, CA
Dawn Picollelli, Wilmington, DE
Gail Weidner, Tustin, CA
Jane Yeiser Woods, Sarasota, FL

FUN WITH PURPLE

Quick Starts for Purple Day

- Draw on lavender paper with purple felt-tip markers.
- Drink grape juice.
- Glue purple plum shapes on pictures of green trees.
- Spread crackers with peanut butter and grape jelly.
- Pass around an eggplant to touch and examine.
- Read *A Picture for Harold's Room; A Purple Crayon Adventure* by Crockett Johnson.
- Print grapes with carrot rounds and purple paint.
- Make grape Popsicles.
- Shred and taste purple cabbage.
- Experiment with watercolor paints and brushes to discover purple.
- Snack on purple grapes.
- Walk along a piece of rope holding a purple beanbag.
- Dye eggshell pieces purple and use them to create mosaics.
- Touch and smell irises, lilacs and violets.
- Sponge print lilac blossoms using lavender and purple paint.
- Dry purple grapes in a slow oven to make raisins.

Art

PURPLE PEOPLE EATERS

Give each child a purple produce sack from the grocery store with the white handle removed. Set out crayons, felt-tip markers, assorted colors of construction paper scraps and glue. Then let the children decorate their sacks any way they wish to create "one-eyed, one-horned, flying purple people eaters."

Variation: Instead of purple produce sacks, use ordinary grocery bags and let the children paint them purple.

PURPLE YARN PICTURES

Cut 6-inch squares out of white tagboard and cut various shades of purple yarn into short pieces. Have the children brush glue on their tagboard squares. Then let them arrange the yarn pieces on top of the glue to make pictures or designs. When the glue has dried, mount the yarn pictures on 8-inch squares cut from purple construction paper.

Variation: Let the children work together to create a bunch of grapes by gluing small circles of purple yarn on a piece of white tagboard.

TISSUE PAPER VIOLETS

Set out sheets of white construction paper, small bowls of liquid starch and brushes. Give each child a number of violet shapes cut out of purple tissue paper. Have the children brush liquid starch on their papers. Then let them arrange their tissue paper violets on top of the starch.

SHAVING CREAM FINGERPAINT

Give each child a Ziploc sandwich bag filled one-third full with shaving cream. Let the children take turns squeezing drops of red and blue food coloring into their bags before sealing them closed. Then have the children squeeze their bags and watch as the shaving cream turns purple. Let them use their purple shaving cream to fingerpaint designs on sheets of white butcher paper.

Variation: Let the children create flowering trees or lilac bushes by fingerpainting purple blossoms on pictures of bare branches.

PURPLE RAIN

In a hallway or a corner of the room, use sheets of plastic to cover the walls and the floor. Attach pieces of butcher paper or newsprint to the plastic on the walls. Have the children dip large brushes into runny purple paint. Then let them push their brushes against the paper and watch as the "purple rain" comes dripping down.

Hint: Use this activity to combine an April showers theme with a unit on purple.

PURPLE TULIP PRINTS

Cut a number of tulip shapes out of purple tissue paper for each child. Have the children brush white vinegar on sheets of white construction paper. Then let them cover their papers with their tissue paper tulips. As the vinegar dries, the tissue paper will fall off, leaving purple tulip prints.

PLAYDOUGH GRAPES

Make two batches of playdough. Color one batch with red tempera paint and the other with blue. Let the children squeeze lumps of the two colors together to create purple. Then let them roll pieces of the playdough into balls to make grapes.

PURPLE POPCORN FLOWERS

Let the children shake popped popcorn in paper bags to which you have added small amounts of powdered purple tempera paint. Then let them glue the purple popcorn in clusters on sheets of white construction paper to make flowers. When the glue has dried, have the children use crayons or felt-tip markers to add stems and leaves.

Hint: Use this activity in the spring to make lilacs.

SOAP AND WATER FINGERPAINT

Put powdered red and blue tempera paint into separate spice jars (the kind with perforated lids). Give each child a piece of white butcher paper and place a small amount of liquid soap mixed with water in the center. Then let the children sprinkle red and blue paint on top of the soap mixture and use it to fingerpaint designs. As the colors mix, the fingerpaint will turn purple.

PURPLE GRAPE PRINTS

Make a "grapes" stamp for each child by wrapping a piece of tape or a rubber band around three toilet tissue tubes. Make paint pads by placing folded paper towels in shallow containers and pouring on purple paint. Then let the children dip the ends of the toilet tissue tubes into the paint and press them on white construction paper to print bunches of grapes. When the paint has dried, let the children use crayons to add stems and leaves, if desired.

Learning Games

PLANTING TULIPS

Turn a shoebox upside down and cut six slits in the top. Number the slits from 1 to 6 in random order. Cut six tulip shapes out of purple construction paper and number them from 1 to 6 by drawing the corresponding number of dots on each shape. Glue the tulip shapes to Popsicle sticks. Then let the children take turns "planting the tulips" by inserting them into the matching numbered slits in the shoebox.

Science

COLOR MIXING EXPERIMENT

Place three baby food jars on the science table. Fill two of the jars with water and leave the third jar empty. Use food coloring to color the water in one of the jars red and the water in the other jar blue. Place an eyedropper in each jar of water. Then let the children take turns using the eyedroppers to squeeze drops of red and blue water into the empty jar to create purple.

PURPLE CLOVER CHAINS

Take the children on a walk in summertime to pick long-stemmed purple clover. Show them how to string the flowers together in a chain by making a slit in the stem of one flower and pulling the stem of another flower through the slit. Continue the process, seeing how long a chain you can make.

Variation: Let the children pick small handfuls of clover. Then tie each bouquet with a purple yarn bow.

Language

I NEVER SAW A PURPLE COW

Recite the following popular rhyme with the children:

> I never saw a Purple Cow,
> I never hope to see one.
> But I can tell you, anyhow,
> I'd rather see than be one!

Ask the children to pretend that they have indeed seen a purple cow and have them make up a group story about it. Write down the story and then let the children draw pictures to illustrate it. Display the story with the illustrations or staple them together to make a Purple Cow Book.

Variation: Draw a large picture of a cow on butcher paper and let the children paint it purple. Then display the picture on a wall or a bulletin board with the rhyme written below it.

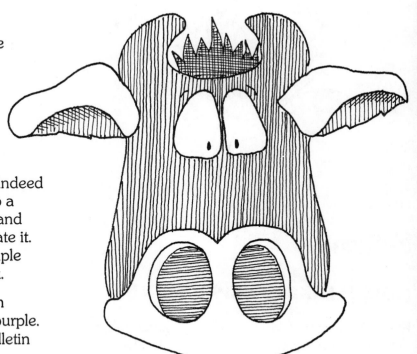

FIVE PURPLE POLKA DOTS

Let the children take turns acting out the movements as they recite the following rhyme:

> Five purple polka dots lay on the floor,
> One sat up and then there were four.
> Four purple polka dots got on their knees,
> One tipped over and then there were three.
> Three purple polka dots stood on one shoe,
> One fell down and then there were two.
> Two purple polka dots started to run,
> One stopped quickly and then there was one.
> One purple polka dot rolled toward the door,
> When it disappeared there were no more.

Janet Hoffman
Elmira, NY

Music

I MET A PURPLE COW
Sung to: "Little White Duck"

I met a purple cow,
Walking down the street.
A little purple cow,
With purple eyes and feet.
She looked just like the other cows do,
Except she was purple and her milk was, too.
I met a purple cow,
Walking down the street.
Moo, moo, moo.

Jean Warren

LITTLE JACK HORNER
Sung to: "Alouette"

Little Jack, Little Jack Horner,
Sat eating his Christmas pie.
He put in his little thumb,
Pulled out a purple plum.
Purple plum, purple plum,
Purple plum, purple plum, oh—
Little Jack, eating Christmas pie,
Said, "What a good boy am I!"

Jean Warren

Movement

PURPLE SHAPE PARADE

Cut large shapes out of purple construction paper and tape them to the floor. Then let the children walk, march, hop, etc., across the shapes as you play music. Tie purple crepe paper streamers to the children's wrists to add to the fun, if desired.

Variation: Let the children bounce balls on the shapes or use them as "stepping stones" in a start-to-finish game.

Snacks

PURPLE COWS

Pour 1 quart milk and 1 6-ounce can unsweetened frozen grape juice concentrate into a plastic container that has a tightly fitting lid. Then let the children take turns shaking the container until the milk and grape juice are well mixed. Pour into clear plastic glasses and serve. Makes 9 to 10 servings.

THUMB PIES

In a mixing bowl, blend together 1 cup flour, ½ teaspoon salt, 4 tablespoons margarine and 2 tablespoons water. Form dough into little balls and make a deep thumbprint in each ball. Place on a cookie sheet and bake at 350 degrees for 20 to 25 minutes. When cool, fill the thumbprint holes with grape jelly. Makes 16 to 18 pies.

PURPLE FLUFF

Pour ¼ cup water into a bowl and sprinkle on 2 envelopes unflavored gelatin. Stir and let set for 5 minutes. Add ¾ cup boiling water and stir until gelatin is dissolved. Pour mixture into a blender container and add 1 6-ounce can unsweetened frozen grape juice concentrate. Blend well and pour into small cups. Chill for about 15 minutes. Makes 4 small servings.

For additional activities that can be used to teach the color purple, see "Fun With Many Colors," beginning on p. 79.

Ideas in this chapter were contributed by:

Valerie Bielsker, Lenexa, KS
Annette Delaney, Houston, TX
Cindy Dingwall, Palatine, IL
Cathy Griffin, Princeton Junction, NJ
Kim Heckert, Adrian, MI
Janet Hoffman, Elmira, NY
Colraine Pettipaw Hunley, Doylestown, PA
Julie Israel, Bloomington, IL

Barb Johnson, Decorah, IA
Elizabeth A. Lokensgard, Appleton, WI
Alice Marks, Roseville, MN
Susan A. Miller, Kutztown, PA
Kathy Monahan, Coon Rapids, MN
Susan Peters, Upland, CA
Elaine Wandschneider, Spokane, WA

FUN WITH BROWN

Quick Starts for Brown Day

- Print with leaf-shaped cookie cutters and different shades of brown paint.
- Glue scraps of wood together to make sculptures.
- Fingerpaint with chocolate pudding.
- Go outside to dig for earthworms.
- Snack on brown wheat crackers or whole-wheat toast.
- Read stories about brown bears.
- Mix different colors of paint together to discover brown.
- Eat pancakes topped with maple syrup.
- Create with playdough that has been sprinkled with cinnamon.
- Fingerpaint brown designs on trays and blot with teddy bear shapes.
- Make gingerbread.
- Create a Potato Man puppet and make up stories about his adventures.
- Glue brown feathers on brown bird shapes.
- Paint wiggly worms with strings dipped in brown paint.
- Fingerpaint with shaving cream on brown butcher paper or brown paper bags.
- Use brown cardboard cartons for stacking and building.
- Print with potato halves and brown paint.

Art

GINGERBREAD PEOPLE

Give each of the children a large gingerbread person shape cut from brown construction paper. Let them use Q-Tip applicators and glue to attach raisins for eyes and small pieces of red pipe cleaners for mouths. Then let them decorate the bodies of their shapes by gluing on rickrack, buttons, fabric circles, bows, etc.

Variation: Cut the gingerbread people out of brown grocery bags instead of construction paper.

TEXTURED BASKETS

Draw basket shapes on 8½- by 11-inch sheets of white paper. Let the children take turns placing their basket pictures on top of a piece of latch hook canvas and rubbing across them with a brown crayon. Have them cut out their textured baskets and glue them on large sheets of construction paper. Then let them tear or cut out magazine pictures of brown things to glue in their baskets.

Variation: Let the children work together to color an extra-large sheet of paper brown. Then cut the paper into a basket shape and mount it on a wall or a bulletin board to hold works of art that the children create.

BROWN TREE PRINTS

Paint each child's palm and arm (up to the elbow) with brown tempera paint. Then have the children press their arms and hands (with fingers apart) on sheets of white construction paper to make bare tree prints. When the paint has dried, let the children glue on crumpled squares of brown tissue paper to make leaves.

BROWN AUTUMN LEAVES

Take a walk with the children to gather dry brown autumn leaves. When you get back, let the children brush glue on large brown construction paper leaf shapes. Then let them crumble the dry leaves and sprinkle the pieces on top of the glue.

BROWN FURRY BEARS

Cut free-form shapes out of brown fake fur for the children to use as bear bodies. Have the children glue their shapes on sheets of white construction paper. Then let them use brown felt-tip markers to add heads, legs and any other details they wish. If desired, provide the children with plastic moving eyes to glue on their bear faces. (Both fake fur and plastic moving eyes are available at craft stores.)

BROWN LEAF RUBBINGS

Place foil cupcake liners in a muffin tin and fill them with peeled pieces of old brown crayons. Then melt the crayon pieces in a slow oven to make large chunky crayons. When the crayons have cooled, peel off the cupcake liners. At art time, have the children arrange leaves on a tabletop and cover them with sheets of thin white paper. Then let them rub the chunky brown crayons over their papers to make leaf rubbings.

Variation: Use ordinary brown crayons instead of large chunky ones.

BROWN FOOTBALLS

Cut football shapes out of brown construction paper. Then let the children use white crayons to draw laces down the centers of their shapes and stripes on the ends.

Variation: For a fun lacing activity, fold each football shape in half lengthwise and use a hole punch to punch a row of holes about 1 inch in from the fold. Then open the shapes and let the children lace white yarn through the holes.

BROWN COLLAGES

Make backgrounds by attaching sheets of light and dark brown construction paper to pieces of lightweight cardboard. Set out glue and a variety of brown items (brown fabric scraps, brown buttons, brown yarn, etc.). Then let the children glue the items on their backgrounds to create brown collages.

SPICY NECKLACES

Cut 3-inch squares out of brown sandpaper and set out pieces of cinnamon sticks. Let the children use the cinnamon stick pieces to "color" on their sandpaper squares. When they have finished, punch a hole in the top of each square and tie on a loop of brown yarn. Then let the children enjoy sniffing the spicy sandpaper while wearing their necklaces.

PEANUT BUTTER PLAYDOUGH

Mix together equal amounts of peanut butter and dry nonfat milk to make playdough (add more peanut butter or dry milk as needed). Wash cookie cutters and any other playing utensils you wish to use and set them out on a clean tabletop. Then invite the children to touch, smell, taste and create with this different kind of playdough.

Variation: For a sweeter taste, mix together ½ large jar peanut butter and ¼ cup honey. Add dry milk until the mixture is the consistency of playdough.

Learning Games

FLANNELBOARD FUN

Cut a variety of sizes of teddy bear shapes out of brown felt. Then let the children arrange the shapes on the flannelboard from smallest to largest.

Variation: Use the teddy bear shapes for counting. Sing "Ten Little Teddy Bears" to the tune of "Ten Little Indians" and let the children take turns placing one shape at a time on the flannelboard.

Language

BROWN MYSTERY BAGS

Give each child a brown paper lunch bag to take home. Attach a note asking parents to help the child place something brown in the bag to bring back the next day for a language experience. At circle time, let each child describe the brown object inside his or her bag without naming it. Have the child continue giving descriptive clues until the others guess what it is.

Hint: This activity works best with small groups.

BROWN LOTTO

Make a gameboard by dividing a sheet of white tagboard into six or more squares. Glue a different brown construction paper shape in each square (a teddy bear, a gingerbread man, a shoe, a cookie, a horse, a worm, etc.). Make game cards by gluing matching shapes on six or more small tagboard squares. Then let the children take turns placing the cards on top of the matching squares on the gameboard.

Variation: Use brown picture stickers instead of construction paper shapes.

THE GINGERBREAD MAN

Read or tell the story of the Gingerbread Man. Then let the children help make gingerbread man cookies and put them in the oven to bake. Arrange to have another adult take the cookies out of the oven when they are done and hide them in a predetermined location. When the children return to the kitchen and see that the cookies have disappeared, let them discover this note on the oven door: "Run, run, as fast as you can. You can't catch me, I'm the Gingerbread Man!" With the children, check in various rooms or areas to find clues that you have written on brown gingerbread man shapes. Then follow the clues until the cookies have been found and let the children enjoy them as snacks.

Science

SORTING NUTS

Provide the children with a variety of unshelled nuts (pecans, Brazil nuts, peanuts, almonds, walnuts, etc.). Discuss the brown shades of the nutshells and have the children sort the nuts into groups, ranging from lightest to darkest brown. If desired, crack open a few of the nuts for tasting.

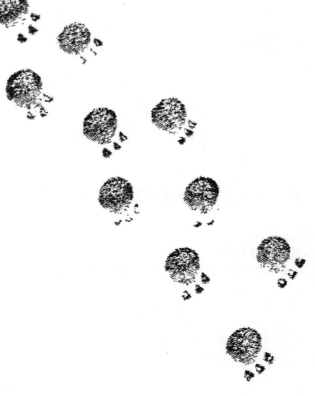

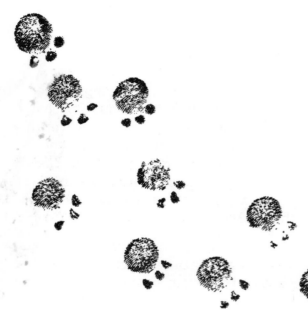

BROWN NATURE WALK

Take the children on a "brown discovery walk." Have them collect small brown items (twigs, dry leaves, seeds, etc.) and place them in brown paper lunch bags to use later for a group collage. Or take along a piece of cardboard and a small bottle of glue and attach brown items to the cardboard as they are discovered (this method helps limit the size and number of "finds").

FUN WITH MUD

Let the children enjoy an outdoor "messy experience" with a tub of brown mud. Have them observe as you gradually add water to dirt and let them squeeze the squishy mixture through their fingers. Let them try fingerpainting with the mud. Then let them experiment with adding more dirt until the mud can be molded into shapes. While the children are creating, let them sing the following silly song to the tune of "If You're Happy and You Know It":

> Oh, I wish I were a little hunk of mud,
> Oh, I wish I were a little hunk of mud.
> Then I'd ooey and I'd gooey
> Over everybody's shoey.
> Oh, I wish I were a little hunk of mud.

Author Unknown

Music

BROWN LEAVES
Sung to: "Twinkle, Twinkle, Little Star"

Brown leaves, brown leaves, all around,
Twirling, swirling to the ground.
See them dancing through the air,
See them falling everywhere.
Brown leaves, brown leaves, all around,
Twirling, swirling to the ground.

Jean Warren

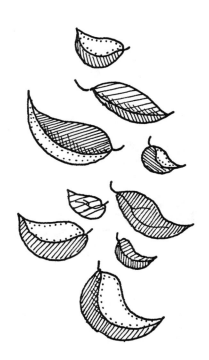

THREE BROWN BEARS
Sung to: "Three Blind Mice"

Three brown bears, three brown bears.
See all their beds, see all their chairs.
The mommy cooked in a big brown pot,
The daddy's porridge was much too hot,
The baby bear always cried a lot.
Three brown bears.

Judith E. McNitt
Adrian, MI

Movement

HOT POTATO

Have the children sit on the floor in a circle and give one child a potato. Then play music and have the children pass the "hot" potato around the circle as fast as they can so that it doesn't "burn" their fingers. When you stop the music, have the child who is holding the potato stand up, twirl around and then sit down again. Continue the game as long as interest lasts.

Snacks

PEANUT BUTTER

Let the children help shell a package of unsalted roasted peanuts. Then let them grind the peanuts in a food grinder. Mix the ground nuts with ½ cube softened margarine and add salt to taste. Spread on brown crackers or slices of whole-wheat bread.

NUTS & BOLTS

Place 4 cups bite-sized shredded wheat in a baking pan in one layer. Drizzle on ⅓ cup melted margarine and sprinkle with a little garlic powder. Bake at 350 degrees for 15 minutes. When cool, add 1½ cups stick pretzels (broken in half), ½ cup raisins and ½ cup dry roasted peanuts. Mix well and store in an airtight container.

BROWN BEAR SANDWICHES

Let the children use a cookie cutter to cut heart shapes out of slices of whole-wheat bread. Show them how to cut the points off their hearts to make the shapes resemble bear faces. Have the children spread peanut butter on their bear face shapes. Then let them use raisins to make eyes and mouths and cherries or unsweetened berries to make noses.

For additional activities that can be used to teach the color brown, see "Fun With Many Colors," beginning on p. 79.

For additional activities that can be used to teach the color brown, see "Fun With Many Colors," beginning on p. 79.

Ideas in this chapter were contributed by:

Deborah Balmer, Mesa, AZ
Valerie Bielsker, Lenexa, KS
Tamara Clohessy, Weaverville, CA
Cathy Griffin, Princeton Junction, NJ
Peggy Hanley, St. Joseph, MI
Kim Heckert, Adrian, MI
Nancy J. Heimark, Grand Forks, ND
Colraine Pettipaw Hunley, Doylestown, PA
Barbara H. Jackson, Denton, TX

Barb Johnson, Decorah, IA
Elizabeth A. Lokensgard, Appleton, WI
Kathy Monahan, Coon Rapids, MN
Bonnie Rogers, Olympia, WA
Nancy Ridgeway, Bradford, PA
Karen Seehusen, Fort Dodge, IA
Rosemary Spatafora, Pleasant Ridge, MI
Nancy C. Windes, Denver, CO

FUN WITH BLACK

Quick Starts for Black Day

- Draw pictures with charcoal.

- Count how many in the group have black hair.

- Snack on raisins.

- Bring in a black spider and learn the nursery rhyme "Little Miss Muffet."

- Make prints with a black ink pad and a variety of rubber stamps.

- Use black licorice sticks for straws at snack time.

- Act out the fingerplay "Eensy, Weensy Spider."

- Discuss what happens to your tongue when you eat a black jelly bean.

- Sort black buttons or pebbles by size.

- Print wheels on pictures of cars with spools and black paint.

- Make "burnt match" snacks by placing black pitted olives on the ends of carrot sticks.

- Learn the nursery rhyme "Sing a Song of Sixpence."

- Make copies of pencil drawings using black carbon paper.

- Paint toilet tissue tubes black and tape them together to make binoculars.

- Make texture collages by gluing scraps of black sandpaper, black velvet, black plastic, etc., on black paper plates.

Art

SPIDER WEBS

Cut squares out of white cardboard and make slits around the edges. Tape a piece of black yarn to the back of each square and pull it through one of the slits. Then have the children cross the yarn back and forth over the fronts of their cardboard squares, attaching it through the slits (slits can be used more than once). Let them continue until their yarn creations resemble spider webs. Then trim the ends of the yarn and tape them to the backs of the squares.

CLOTHESPIN BATS

Have the children paint spring-type clothespins black to use as bat bodies. When the paint has dried, give each of the children a bat wings shape cut from black construction paper and have them glue their shapes on their clothespins. Then clip the bats around the room on curtains, picture frames, book covers, etc.

FUZZY BLACK CATS

Mix cornmeal with powdered black tempera paint and pour it into shaker containers. Cut cat shapes out of black construction paper. Have the children brush glue on their shapes and place them in shallow box lids. Then let them sprinkle the black cornmeal on top of the glue and shake off the excess.

Variation: Use salt instead of cornmeal.

BLACK TRIANGLE COLLAGES

Use white chalk to draw large triangle shapes on sheets of black construction paper. Have the children cut out the shapes. Then let them decorate their triangles by gluing on a variety of black items (black magazine pictures, black fabric pieces, black yarn, black glitter, black buttons, black sequins, etc.).

Variation: If you're doing this activity near Halloween, cut the black construction paper into large cat, bat or witch hat shapes.

BLACK HANDPRINTS

Paint the palms of the children's hands black. Then have them press their hands on sheets of tagboard to make handprints. Label the prints "left" and "right" and add the children's names and the date. Then let the children take their handprints home as gifts.

NIGHT SKY PICTURES

Make a night sky "mystery picture" for each child. Use a white crayon to color stars and a moon on a sheet of white construction paper (press down hard with the crayon while coloring). Then let each child brush thinned black tempera paint over his or her paper to reveal the moon and stars shining in the black night sky.

BLACK SHEEP

Read or sing the nursery rhyme "Baa, Baa, Black Sheep" (see p. 69). Give each of the children a sheep shape cut out of white tagboard. Have the children brush glue on their shapes and cover them with white cotton balls. Then let them turn their white sheep into black sheep by sprinkling on powdered black tempera paint and shaking off the excess.

SPOOKY SHAPES

Cut the classified ads sections from old newspapers into squares and set out sheets of black construction paper and glue. Let the children tear the newspaper squares into "spooky shapes" and glue them on their papers. Then let them add more glue and sprinkle on black glitter.

PAPER PLATE SPIDERS

Have the children paint paper plates black to create spider bodies. When the paint has dried, have them each glue four black construction paper strips on one side of their plates and four strips on the other side to make legs. Then let them use white chalk to draw eyes near the tops of their spider bodies.

EGG CARTON SPIDERS

For each child cut an egg cup out of a cardboard egg carton to use as a spider body. Poke four holes in one side of the cup and four holes in the opposite side. Thread a 3-inch length of pipe cleaner through each set of opposite holes and bend down the ends of the pipe cleaners to create eight legs. Let the children paint their spiders black. When the paint has dried, attach rubber band strings to the tops of the spiders so that the children can bounce them up and down.

Learning Games

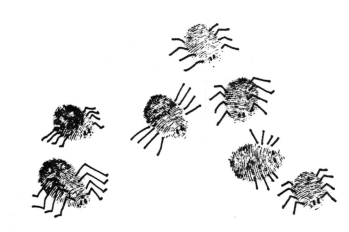

COUNTING JELLY BEANS

For each child divide a piece of paper into four squares and write the numerals 1 to 4 in the squares in random order. Give the children each a paper cup containing ten black jelly beans to count. Then have them place the corresponding number of jelly beans in each numbered square on their papers.

Variation: Use black buttons instead of jelly beans.

Science

COUNTING SPIDER PRINTS

Set out a black ink pad and let the children make fingerprints on white index cards. Then use a black pen to draw eight legs and two eyes on each fingerprint to make spiders (let older children try drawing the legs and eyes themselves). Have each child count the number of spiders on his or her card. Then write the corresponding numeral on the bottom of the card.

Variation: If you wish to use this activity for teaching the number "8," begin by asking each child to make eight fingerprints.

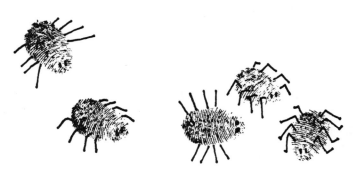

SPIDER DAY

Combine your study of the color black with Spider Day. Bring in a black spider for the children to examine and observe. Talk about what spiders do and how they can be distinguished from insects (spiders have eight legs; insects have six). At the end of the day, go outside with the children and set the spider free.

SILHOUETTES

Use black construction paper to make a silhouette of each child from a shadow cast on a wall. Display the silhouettes on a bulletin board and let the children try to guess who's who. Use this activity to discuss shadows and how they are created.

Movement

STUFF THE PILLOW

Have the children sit in a circle and give them each a pile of newspaper squares. Place a black plastic trash bag in the middle of the circle. Have the children crumple the newspaper squares and stuff them into the trash bag. When the bag is full, let the children take turns jumping on their big black "pillow."

Language

LITTLE SHADOW

Let the children act out the movements as you recite the poem below.

> There is a little shadow
> That dances on my wall.
> Sometimes it's big and scary,
> Sometimes it's very small.
>
> Sometimes it's oh, so quiet
> And doesn't move at all.
> Then other times it chases me
> Or bounces like a ball.
>
> I'd love to meet that shadow
> Who dances in the night,
> But it always runs away
> When I turn on the light.

Jean Warren

TWO LITTLE BLACKBIRDS

Let the children wear little cones of black construction paper taped to the tops of their index fingers while they act out the fingerplay below.

Two little blackbirds
Sitting on a hill.
    (Hold up both index fingers.)
One named Jack,
    (Wiggle one finger.)
The other named Jill.
    (Wiggle other finger.)
Fly away, Jack.
    (Put first finger behind back.)
Fly away, Jill.
    (Put other finger behind back.)
Come back, Jack.
    (Return first finger to front.)
Come back, Jill.
    (Return other finger to front.)

Traditional

Music

I SEE SHADOWS
Sung to: "Skip to My Lou"

I see shadows on the wall,
I see shadows on the wall,
I see shadows on the wall.
Some are big and some are small.

Watch them move like I do,
    (Raise arms high.)
Watch them move like I do,
    (Lower arms.)
Watch them move like I do.
    (Crouch down low.)
I pop up and they do, too!
    (Jump up.)

Let groups of children take turns being "shadows" and
imitating the movements of the other children as they sing.

Jean Warren

BLACK BEAR, BLACK BEAR
Sung to: "Twinkle, Twinkle, Little Star"

Black bear, black bear, turn around,
Black bear, black bear, touch the ground.
Black bear, black bear, reach up high,
Black bear, black bear, touch the sky.
Black bear, black bear, reach down low,
Black bear, black bear, touch your toe.

Additional verse: "Black cat, black cat, turn around."

Adapted Traditional

BAA, BAA, BLACK SHEEP
Sung to: "Twinkle, Twinkle, Little Star"

Baa, baa, black sheep,
Have you any wool?
Yes sir, yes sir,
Three bags full.
    (Hold up three fingers.)
One for my master,
    (Hold up one finger.)
One for the dame,
    (Hold up two fingers.)
And one for the little boy
    (Hold up three fingers.)
Who lives down the lane.
Baa, baa, black sheep,
Have you any wool?
Yes sir, yes sir,
Three bags full.
    (Hold up three fingers.)

Adapted Traditional

Snacks

PRUNE SPIDERS

Give each of the children a large soft prune to use as a spider body. Then let them poke pretzel sticks or crispy Chinese noodles into the sides of their prunes to make legs.

ANTS-ON-A-LOG

Let the children help make "logs" by filling celery sticks with peanut butter. Then give them each three or four raisin "ants" to place on top of their logs.

Variation: For a different kind of stuffing have the children mix together equal portions of peanut butter, grated carrots and crushed shredded wheat. Let them press the mixture into celery sticks and then place raisins on top.

For additional activities that can be used to teach the color black, see "Fun With Many Colors," beginning on p. 79.

Ideas in this chapter were contributed by:

Valerie Bielsker, Lenexa, KS
Cindy Davis, Finleyville, PA
Sandra England, Kirkland, WA
Barb Johnson, Decorah, IA
Elizabeth A. Lokensgard, Appleton, WI
Joleen Meier, Marietta, GA

Susan A. Miller, Kutztown, PA
Kathy Monahan, Coon Rapids, MN
Donna Mullennix, Thousand Oaks, CA
Bonnie Rogers, Olympia, WA
Mary Whaley, Kentland, IN

FUN WITH WHITE

Quick Starts for White Day

- String macaroni on white yarn to make necklaces.
- Fingerpaint with white shaving cream.
- Go outside to watch white clouds in the sky.
- Make mashed potatoes.
- Dip string in white glue and arrange it in designs on white Styrofoam food trays.
- Sing the song "Little White Duck."
- Use white Styrofoam packing pieces for sandbox play.
- Draw on dark colored paper with white chalk.
- Serve milk, white bread or plain yogurt at snack time.
- Toss "snowballs" made of crumpled sheets of white paper.
- Use a bar of Ivory Soap as a floating toy.
- Taste grated coconut.
- Play with white tennis balls or white plastic golf balls.
- Make white collages by gluing white facial tissues, pasta shapes, cotton balls, etc., on white paper plates.
- Twist white pipe cleaners into freeform shapes.
- Glue stretched-out cotton balls on light blue construction paper to make cloud pictures.

Art

SNOW SCENES

Whip Ivory Snow powder with water until the mixture is soft and fluffy. Let the children fingerpaint with the soap mixture on sheets of heavy white paper or tagboard. While the mixture is still wet, let them add Styrofoam packing pieces for snowflakes and cotton balls for clouds. Then let them sprinkle on silver glitter to add sparkle to their snow scenes.

EGGSHELL HUMPTY DUMPTYS

Recite the nursery rhyme "Humpty Dumpty" and pass around an unshelled hard-boiled egg for the children to examine. Set out egg shapes cut from white construction paper, glue and small bowls of broken eggshells. Then let the children glue the eggshells on their egg shapes to create cracked Humpty Dumptys. When they have finished, give them each two plastic moving eyes (available at craft stores) to glue on their egg shapes.

COTTON BALL LAMBS

For each child cut the shape of a lamb's head and body out of white tagboard or lightweight cardboard. Set out cotton balls, glue and black felt-tip markers. Recite the nursery rhyme "Mary Had a Little Lamb." Then let the children draw eyes and ears on their lamb shapes and glue on cotton balls to create "fleece as white as snow." When the glue has dried, clip two spring-type clothespins on the bottom of each shape to make legs for the fluffy lambs to stand on.

SHOE POLISH CLOUDS

Set out sheets of light blue construction paper and bottles of white liquid shoe polish (the kind with sponge applicators). Let the children use the shoe polish to draw clouds on their papers. Then mount the pictures on a wall or a bulletin board and let the children discuss what they think the cloud shapes look like.

73

SNOW-COVERED EVERGREENS

Provide the children with cone-shaped paper cups (check a local restaurant supply store for cups used to hold Sno Cones). Have the children turn their paper cups upside down and paint them green. Then let them sprinkle Ivory Snow powder over the wet paint to create snow-covered evergreen trees.

POPCORN SNOWMEN

Let the children help make a big batch of popcorn. Cut snowman shapes out of white construction paper or tagboard and pour glue into shallow containers. Then let the children dip the popcorn pieces into the glue and place them all over their snowman shapes. If desired, let them add facial features torn or cut from black construction paper.

SNOWFLAKE PRINTS

Cut green peppers in half horizontally and clean out the seeds. Make paint pads by placing folded paper towels in shallow containers and pouring on white tempera paint. Then let the children dip the pepper halves into the paint and press them on sheets of dark colored construction paper to make snowflake prints.

TISSUE PAPER GHOSTS

Cut ghost shapes out of white construction paper and tear white tissue paper into small pieces. Have the children brush liquid starch on their ghost shapes and arrange the torn tissue paper on top of the starch. Then have them brush more starch on top of the tissue pieces. When the starch has dried, let the children glue black construction paper eyes on their ghosts.

WHITE SCULPTURES

Give each child a chunk of white Styrofoam to use as a base. Have the children stick white pipe cleaners into their Styrofoam chunks. Then let them decorate the pipe cleaners by threading on a variety of white items (white plastic straw sections, white buttons, white macaroni, white paper doily pieces, etc.).

PLAYING WITH "PUD"

Pour about half a box of cornstarch into a shallow baking pan. Add water slowly and have the children stir the mixture with their fingers to make "Pud." Then let them scoop up handfuls of the mixture, squeeze it and watch what happens.

Hint: The Pud can be used over and over again. Just add more water when the mixture becomes too dry.

Learning Games

WRITING TRAYS

Spread salt on smooth plastic trays. Then let the children use their fingers to write letters or numerals in the salt (older children can write short spelling words). Have the children gently shake the trays when they wish to start over again.

Variation: Instead of salt, use fine white sand (available at most nurseries).

Science

SNOWFLAKES

Display pictures of snowflakes for the children to examine. Explain that snowflakes are frozen water crystals, each with six sides, and that no two are ever alike. If you live in an area where it snows, set out squares of black construction paper or felt to catch real snowflakes (chill the squares beforehand for the best results). Then let the children examine the snowflakes with a magnifying glass.

BRUSHING TEETH

Cut large tooth shapes out of white construction paper or tagboard. Talk about the importance of brushing teeth and how it should be done. Then let the children use old toothbrushes to "brush" their tooth shapes with white tempera paint "toothpaste." Show them how to brush up and down, back and forth and in a circular motion.

Hint: This activity provides excellent practice for the real thing, but stress that the brushes and the pretend toothpaste should not be put into real mouths.

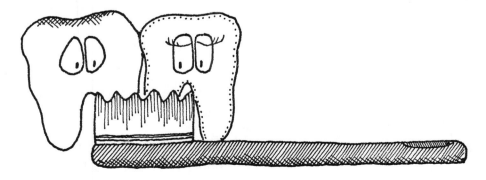

Language

GHOST FINGER PUPPETS

Cut ghost shapes out of small white index cards. Add eyes with a black felt-tip marker and cut two finger holes at the bottom of each shape. Show the children how to make legs for their ghost puppets by sticking two fingers through the finger holes. Then recite the rhyme below, each time naming a different action, and let the children act out the movements with their puppets.

> Little ghost, little ghost,
> Dressed in white,
> See how you (dance/skip/run/etc.)
> On Halloween night.

Jean Warren

Movement

HERE COMES JACK FROST

Have the children stand in a circle. Ask them to name some of their favorite things to do in winter. Then choose one child to be Jack Frost and have the child wait in a corner of the room or just outside the door. Ask the other children to pretend that they are each doing one of the winter activities mentioned. As they are "making snowmen" or "skiing down a hill" have Jack Frost come back and move among the children, trying to touch them as he or she goes. Whenever Jack Frost touches someone, have the child "freeze" and stay in the same position without moving. Let the last child to be touched become the new Jack Frost. Then have the children act out different winter activities and repeat the game.

Hint: Make an "icy crown" for Jack Frost by cutting the center out of a paper plate and decorating the rim with white crepe paper strips.

Music

EASTER BUNNY
Sung to: "Twinkle, Twinkle, Little Star"

Easter Bunny soft and white,
Hopping quickly out of sight.
Thank you for the eggs you bring,
At Eastertime we welcome spring.
Easter Bunny soft and white,
Hopping quickly out of sight.

Irmgard Fuertges
Kitchener, Ontario

SNOWFLAKES FALLING DOWN
Sung to: "Row, Row, Row Your Boat"

Snowflakes falling down,
(Lower hands while fluttering fingers.)
Falling to the ground.
Big, white fluffy flakes
(Make circles with thumbs and index fingers.)
That do not make a sound.
(Put finger to lips and shake head.)

Susan A. Miller
Kutztown, PA

BRUSH YOUR TEETH
Sung to: "Row, Row, Row Your Boat"

Brush, brush, brush your teeth
Till they're clean and white.
Brush them, brush them,
Brush them, brush them,
Morning, noon and night.

Paula Schneider
Kent, WA

POPCORN POPPING
Sung to: "Old MacDonald Had a Farm"

Popcorn popping, oh, what fun,
Popping big and white.
We will wait until it's done,
Then we'll grab a bite.
With a pop, pop here,
And a pop, pop there,
Here a pop, there a pop,
Everywhere a pop, pop.
Popcorn popping, oh, what fun,
Popping big and white.

Elizabeth McKinnon

Snacks

COTTAGE CHEESE DIP

Whirl cottage cheese in a blender and add sour cream or milk to make a thick creamy mixture. Flavor to taste with your favorite white salad dressing. Refrigerate for 30 minutes. Then serve with raw vegetables such as cauliflower florets or cucumber spears.

POPCORN SNOWFALL

Place a hot air popcorn popper on a clean white sheet that has been spread out on the floor. Add popcorn kernels and plug in the popper, leaving the top off. Have the children sit back from the popper and watch as the corn pops and falls like snow. Then let them eat the popcorn for a snack.

Caution: Activities that involve using an electric appliance require adult supervision at all times.

For additional activities that can be used to teach the color white, see "Fun With Many Colors," beginning on p. 79.

Ideas in this chapter were contributed by:

Valerie Bielsker, Lenexa, KS
Cindy Davis, Finleyville, PA
Marjorie Debowy, Stony Brook, NY
Cathy Griffin, Princeton Junction, NJ
Peggy Hanley, St. Joseph, MI
Kim Heckert, Adrian, MI
Colraine Pettipaw Hunley, Doylestown, PA

Elizabeth A. Lokensgard, Appleton, WI
Susan A. Miller, Kutztown, PA
Bonnie Rogers, Olympia, WA
Kathy Sizer, Tustin, CA
Gail Weidner, Tustin, CA
Anne Lemay Zipf, Metuchen, NJ

FUN WITH MANY COLORS

Quick Starts for
Any Color Day

- Dress in clothes that are the Color of the Day.
- Add the desired color of food coloring to playdough and set it out on the art table.
- Take a walk to look for a particular color of car.
- Dip cooked spaghetti in the desired color of paint and let it "dance" across white paper.
- Make a chart listing foods that are the Color of the Day.
- String the desired color of buttons on matching colored telephone wire to make necklaces.
- Use paper plates and napkins that are the Color of the Day for snack time.
- Try guessing how many of the same colored buttons, beads, etc., there are in a glass jar, then count to see who came closest.
- Add food coloring to white glue to coordinate with the Color of the Day.
- Mix cream cheese with the desired color of fruit or vegetable bits (tomatoes, pineapple, blueberries, etc.) and spread on crackers for snacks.
- Plan a scavenger hunt to search for objects that are the desired color.
- Freeze water tinted with the desired color of food coloring in milk cartons to make ice sculptures for the water table.
- Use the desired color of paper cups for stacking in pyramids or for counting.
- Make finger Jell-O to coordinate with the Color of the Day.
- Tint rice with the desired color of food coloring to use for sandbox play.

Art

COLOR CHAINS

At the beginning of each month, cut sheets of the desired color of construction paper into a number of 1- by 6-inch strips. Then during free time, let the children use the strips to create a long paper chain. When they have finished, mount the chain on a bulletin board in an appropriate shape (a red apple for September, an orange pumpkin for October, a white snowman for January, etc.). The children will enjoy doing this activity, and you will have an attractive seasonal decoration for your bulletin board each month.

COLOR CROWNS

Let the children make crowns to wear when you celebrate a Color Day. If your selected color is yellow, cut crown shapes out of large sheets of yellow construction paper (or use smaller sheets of construction paper taped together). Then have the children search through magazines for yellow pictures to tear out and glue on their crowns. When they have finished, tape the ends of each crown together in the back.

BALLOON COLLAGES

Cut a large balloon shape out of a selected color of construction paper. Have the children glue on magazine pictures that are the same color to create a group collage. Attach the balloon to a wall or a bulletin board and add a matching colored piece of yarn for a balloon string. Repeat the process for each Color Day and by the end of the year, you will have a balloon "rainbow." Attach a big bow to hold all the colored balloon strings together.

GLITTER DOUGH

Use this idea to add sparkle to Color Days or holidays. Make playdough using your favorite recipe. Or combine 1 cup flour, ½ cup salt, 1 cup water, 1 tablespoon vegetable oil and 2 teaspoons cream of tartar. Cook for 3 minutes or until mixture pulls away from pan. Give each child a lump of playdough and sprinkle a selected color of glitter on the tabletop. Then let the children work the glitter into the dough.

CORN SYRUP PAINTING

Pour light corn syrup into three plastic squeeze bottles. Add drops of red food coloring to one bottle, drops of yellow food coloring to another bottle and drops of blue food coloring to the third bottle. Shake the bottles gently, then add more food coloring, if necessary, to create strong bright shades. Let the children squeeze drops of the colored corn syrup on white paper plates. Then have them tip their plates back and forth so that the colors blend and create new colors. Allow the plates to dry for several days.

TIRE TRACKS MURAL

Tape a piece of butcher paper to a tabletop or to the floor. Set out red, yellow and blue toy cars and pour matching colored tempera paints into shallow containers. Then let the children dip the wheels of the colored cars into the matching colored paints and "drive" the cars over the butcher paper to make tracks. Encourage them to crisscross the tracks to create new colors. When the paint has dried, display the mural on a wall or a bulletin board.

MULTICOLORED COLLAGES

Cut red, yellow and blue cellophane into desired shapes. Have the children glue the shapes on sheets of waxed paper, overlapping the edges of the cellophane as they glue. Attach construction paper frames to the collages, if desired. Then hang them in a window to let the light shine through all the colors.

NO-MESS COLOR MIXING

For each child put a small amount of red liquid tempera paint and a small amount of yellow into a Ziploc sandwich bag. Seal the bags closed. Then let the children squeeze their bags to mix the colors and create orange. Follow the same procedure using blue and yellow paint to make green, and red and blue paint to make purple.

Variation: Mix red and white paint to make pink; mix red, yellow and blue paint to make brown.

GUMBALL MACHINES

Give each of the children a gumball machine shape cut from white tagboard and a number of small circles cut from the desired color of construction paper. Have the children color the bottom parts of their gumball machine shapes with crayons or felt-tip markers. Then let them fill the top parts with "gumballs" by gluing on their colored paper circles.

Variation: Use colored circle stickers instead of construction paper circles.

SOAP HOLDER PRINTS

Set out sheets of white construction paper and several soap bar holders (the kind with small suction cups on the bottom). Make paint pads by placing sponges or folded paper towels in shallow containers and pouring on the desired color of tempera paint. Then let the children dip the bottoms of the soap holders into the paint and press them on their papers to make prints.

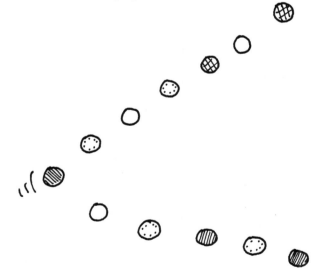

COLORED SPIRALS

Cut large circles out of a selected color of construction paper. Use a wide black felt-tip marker to draw a spiral on each circle. Then hand out scissors and let the children cut along the black lines. Attach matching colored pieces of yarn to the spirals. Then hang them from the ceiling and watch them twirl in the breeze.

Variation: Have the children brush the desired color of paint on both sides of paper plates. When the paint has dried, cut the plates into spirals and attach yarn hangers.

FLOUR AND WATER PAINT

Fill squeeze bottles with a runny mixture of flour and water. Add the desired color of tempera paint or food coloring. Then let the children squeeze the colored flour and water mixture in designs on Styrofoam food trays or squares of tagboard.

83

PLASTER SCULPTURES

Give each child a small plastic bag containing dry quick-setting plaster. Add a selected color of powdered tempera paint and enough water to make a soft dough. Then let the children gently squeeze their bags to mix the plaster, paint and water together. When the plaster feels warm, it will begin to set. Have the children hold their bags in desired shapes until the plaster hardens. Then let them remove their colored sculptures from their plastic bags.

COLORED CLOUD DOUGH

In a large bowl, mix 6 cups flour with the desired color and amount of powdered tempera paint. Add 1½ cups vegetable oil and 1 cup water and knead well. If necessary, add more water in small amounts until the dough is soft and elastic. Then let the children have fun patting, squeezing and pulling the fluffy dough into various shapes. Store dough in the refrigerator in a covered container.

FLOATING ART

Cut white construction paper into seasonal or holiday shapes. Let the children help grate a selected color of chalk into powder by rubbing it against a food grater. Fill a plastic dishpan with water. Then let each child in turn sprinkle some colored chalk powder on the water's surface and place a paper shape on top of the water to absorb the chalk designs. Hang the shapes on a line or lay them out on a flat surface to dry.

COLORFUL BIRD TAILS

For each child draw a picture of a bird (minus the tail) on a sheet of white construction paper. Use crayons or felt-tip markers to draw three or four different colored dots on the back end of the bird. Give each child three or four feather shapes cut from matching colors of construction paper. Then have the children match the feathers with the colored dots and glue the feathers on their birds to make colorful tails. Let them color their bird bodies and add other details with crayons, if desired.

FINGERPAINT BALLOONS

Glue five bottle caps (open ends up) in a semicircle on a piece of heavy cardboard and fill each cap with a different color of tempera paint. Have each child in turn dip all five fingers of one hand into the paint in the bottle caps and then press them on a sheet of white construction paper to make prints. When the paint has dried, let the children draw lines down from their fingerprints, turning them into balloons with strings.

BALLOON PRINTING

Pour three or four different colors of tempera paint into separate aluminum pie tins. Partially blow up a small balloon that matches each paint color. Then have the children dip the balloons into the matching colored paints and press them on sheets of white construction paper to create balloon prints.

Variation: Use just one color of paint and matching colored balloons for individual Color Days.

COLORED MILK PAINTING

Cut egg or flower shapes out of white construction paper. Pour condensed milk (*not* evaporated milk) into small cups and add drops of different colored food coloring. Then let the children use Q-Tips to brush the glossy "paint" on their paper shapes. Encourage them to tip their shapes back and forth to make the colors blend together and create new colors. Place the painted shapes on a flat surface and allow them to dry for several days.

Hint: Condensed milk is expensive, but the colors it produces are so brilliant that you may wish to use it as a once-a-year treat.

COLORED SOAPS

Tint water with a selected color of food coloring and stir it into Ivory Snow powder to make a dough-like mixture (about 2 cups soap powder to ½ cup water). Let the children mold the soap mixture into balls or other shapes and place them on waxed paper to dry. After several days, help the children wrap their soaps in matching colored squares of tissue paper and tie on yarn or ribbon bows. Then let the children take their colored soaps home as gifts.

RAINBOW CRAYONS

Chop assorted colors of old peeled crayons into ¼-inch pieces and place them in a muffin tin that has been lined with foil cupcake liners. Then put the muffin tin into a 400-degree oven for about 5 minutes or until the crayon pieces just begin to melt. Remove the muffin tin before the colors mix together and become muddy. When the crayons have cooled, peel off the cupcake liners. Then let the children use the rainbow crayons for various coloring projects.

COLORS AND FEELINGS

Set out sheets of white construction paper and different colored crayons or felt-tip markers. Talk with the children about various kinds of feelings. Ask them what colors and designs they would use to show happiness, sadness, anger, etc. (accept all responses). Then let them each choose a colored crayon or felt-tip marker and use it to draw a "happy picture." Follow the same procedure to make "sad pictures," "angry pictures," "sleepy pictures," etc.

Variation: Let the children fingerpaint with colors they choose to express feelings.

Learning Games

COLOR DAY TABLE

Try this activity whenever you have a Color Day. Place a sheet of the selected color of construction paper on a tabletop. Then ask each child in turn to find a matching colored object in the room and place it on the table. The children will enjoy watching as the tabletop becomes a sea of color, and they can help if someone chooses a colored object that does not match.

COLOR WHEEL

Cut a 12-inch circle out of white tagboard and divide it into eight sections. Use crayons or felt-tip markers to color each section a different color and draw matching colored dots on eight spring-type clothespins. Then let the children match the colors by clipping the clothespins around the edge of the wheel on the appropriate sections.

COUNTING COLORED DISKS

For each child place six colored plastic disks (available at teacher supply stores) in a plastic sandwich bag. Include two or three of the same colored disks in some of the bags. Have the children sit in a circle. Ask them each to count out their red disks and tell how many they have. Then ask them to place all their red disks in the center of the circle and count with them how many there are all together. Follow the same procedure to count the remaining colors.

COLOR-OF-THE-WEEK BOX

When you are working on a particular color, make a Color-of-the-Week Box. Paint the box the desired color or cover it with construction paper. Then place a few items in the box to get things started. Throughout the week, encourage the children to find matching colored objects inside or outside the room to put into the box (or ask them to bring small objects from home). Set aside some time each day to go through the box and discover the new additions.

MATCHING MITTENS

Make a gameboard by gluing eight mitten shapes cut from different colors of tagboard on a sheet of white tagboard. Cut out eight matching colored mitten shapes to use as game cards. Tape an envelope for holding the cutout mittens on the back of the board. Then let the children take turns matching the colors by placing the cutouts on top of the corresponding mitten shapes on the gameboard.

COLOR CONCENTRATION

Cut two squares each out of six different colors of construction paper and glue the squares on twelve index cards. Mix up the cards and spread them out face down on a tabletop or on the floor. Let one child begin by turning up two cards. If the colors match, let the child keep the cards. If the colors don't match, have the child replace both cards face down exactly where they were before. Continue the game until all the cards have been matched. Then let the child who ended up with the most cards have the first turn when you start the game again.

COLOR WORM

Cut a large rounded worm shape out of white construction paper or tagboard. Use a black felt-tip marker to draw on facial features and to divide the worm into six or more sections. Use crayons or felt-tip markers to color the areas on opposite sides of each dividing line a different color. Cover the worm shape with clear Con-Tact paper, cut out the sections and mix them up. Then let the children take turns piecing the worm together by matching the colors on the ends of the sections.

COLOR CLIPS

Cut 6-inch squares out of three or more different colors of tagboard. Paint four spring-type clothespins to match each square. Mix up the clothespins and place them in a box or a basket. Then let the children match the colors by clipping the clothespins to the sides of the appropriate squares.

COLOR CIRCLES

Use red, yellow and blue yarn to form three circles on a carpet (or cut circles out of construction paper). Set out red, yellow and blue wooden beads. Then let the children sort the beads by placing them inside the matching colored circles.

Hint: To aid in small muscle development, let the children sort the beads with kitchen tongs.

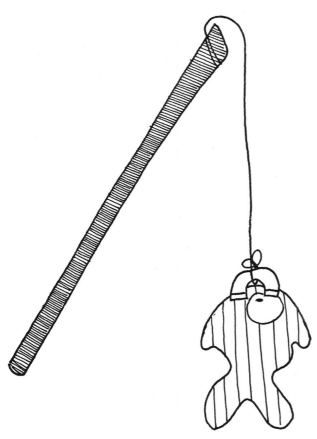

COLOR PUZZLES

Have the children use two or more selected colors to make pictures on large sheets of construction paper. When they have finished, cut each child's picture into three or four puzzle pieces. Then let the children put their own pictures back together, using the colors and shapes of the puzzle pieces as guides.

COLOR FISH

Use a cardboard paper towel tube and a piece of string to make a fishing pole. Tie a small magnet on the end of the string. Cut fish shapes out of three or more different colors of construction paper and attach a paper clip to each fish. Then lay the fish shapes out on the floor and let the children take turns catching a red fish, a blue fish, etc., as you give directions. When all the fish have been caught, let the children sort them into piles by color and count how many there are in each pile.

WHAT'S MISSING?

Have the children sit in a circle. In the center of the circle, line up four to six objects that are the same color (an orange, a carrot, an orange crayon, etc.) and name the objects with the children. Have one child close his or her eyes while you take one object from the line and place it in a paper bag. When the other children say, "One, two, three—look and see," have the child open his or her eyes and try guessing which of the objects is missing. Continue the game until everyone has had a turn.

COLOR CLOTHESLINE

Hang a length of clothesline between two chairs and clip clothespins on the line. Cut clothing shapes (pants, shirts, socks, etc.) out of three or more selected colors of fabric and place them in a basket. Then ask the children to hang up just the red clothes, just the yellow clothes, etc. Or hang different colored clothing shapes on the line and ask the children to hang matching colored shapes next to them.

Variation: Paint clothespins to match the colors of the clothing shapes and let the children hang up the blue clothes with the blue clothespins, the green clothes with the green clothespins, etc.

EGG CARTON SHAKE

Cut twelve small circles out of the desired colors of construction paper and glue them in the sections of an egg carton. Put a button inside the carton and close the lid. Then let the children take turns shaking the egg carton, opening it and naming the color on which the button landed.

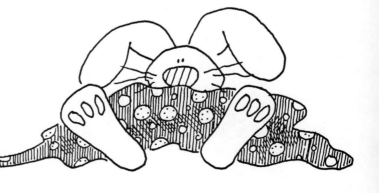

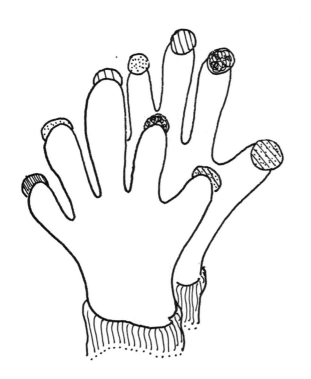

FINGER COLOR MATCHING

Attach different colored circle stickers to the fingertips of the children's right hands and matching colored stickers to the fingertips of their left hands. Have them match up the colors by first putting their two red fingertips together, then their two yellow fingertips, etc. Then let them form in pairs and try matching colored fingertips with their partners.

Variation: Set out objects that match the colors of the circle stickers on the children's fingertips. Then let the children take turns touching a red object with a red finger, a yellow object with a yellow finger, etc.

COLOR CUPS

Color the bottoms of six white cupcake liners different colors and place the liners in a 6-cup muffin tin. Set out an assortment of small matching colored items (beads, buttons, construction paper circles, etc.). Then let the children sort the items by placing them in the matching colored cups.

Variation: Omit the cupcake liners and let the children sort any of the following multicolored items into the muffin tin cups by color: pasta, rubber bands, plastic paper clips, small plastic clothespins, popcorn kernels, plastic toothpicks.

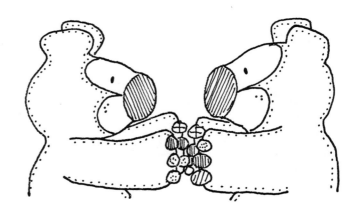

COLOR CORRAL

Divide a shallow box into four different colored sections to make a "color corral." Cut matching colored squares out of construction paper. Then give each of the "color cowboys" and "color cowgirls" a straw and let them take turns sucking up the squares and dropping them into the matching colored sections of the corral.

MATCHING PAINT SAMPLES

Choose a color such as red. At a paint store, pick up two identical paint chip cards that contain samples of red shades. Then cut out the samples, mix them up and let the children find the matching colored pairs. Follow the same procedure when working on other colors.

COLOR CARDS

Use large index cards to make a set of twelve game cards. Make four cards containing red pictures (a red apple, a red wagon, etc.), four cards containing yellow pictures (a yellow banana, a yellow star, etc.) and four cards containing blue pictures (a blue bird, a blue hat, etc.). To play, lay out three cards containing pictures that are the same color and one card containing a picture that is a different color. Then ask the children to identify the different picture and tell why it doesn't belong with the other three.

Variation: Mix up the cards and let the children sort them into groups by color.

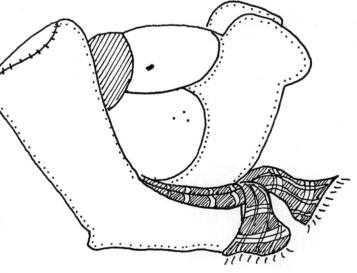

COLOR BOXES

For this game you will need three cigar boxes or shoeboxes without lids. Paint one box red, one yellow and one blue. Provide a tray or a basket containing a variety of red, yellow and blue items (buttons, blocks, small toys, yarn and fabric pieces, etc.). Then let the children sort the items by placing them in the matching colored boxes.

COLOR CUBES

Cut six squares out of different colors of construction paper and insert them in the sides of a plastic photo cube. Cut out six matching colored squares and insert them in the sides of a second photo cube in a different order. Then let the children move the cubes around to find the matching pairs of colors.

Variation: Use one cube as a color die. Let the children take turns rolling the die and then naming the color that comes up.

I SPY

Play this quiet color game whenever you have a few minutes to wait between activities. Have the children glance around the room as you call attention to different colored objects. Then let one child begin by saying, "I spy with my little eye something (red/blue/etc.)." Have the other children try guessing what the colored object is. When a player guesses correctly, let him or her have the next turn.

COLOR MAILBOXES

Make mailboxes by covering the lids of three or more shoeboxes with construction paper and cutting a slit in the top of each lid. Put the lids on the boxes. Draw different colored circles on small index cards and tape them to the backs of the mailboxes so that they stand above the lids. Make "letters" for the mailboxes by drawing matching colored circles on the fronts of sealed envelopes. Then mix up the envelopes and let the children take turns "mailing" them through the slots of the appropriate mailboxes.

COLOR BINGO

Make gameboards by dividing large sheets of white construction paper into eight squares each and drawing different colored circles in the squares. (Use the same eight colors on each gameboard but vary the placement.) Cover the gameboards with clear Con-Tact paper. Then draw matching colored circles on a set of eight index cards. To play, hold up the cards, one at a time, and have the children use crayons to X-out the matching colored circles on their gameboards. When the game is over, wipe the gameboards with a damp paper towel to remove the crayon.

COLOR FOLDER GAME

Make a gameboard by drawing eight different colored bears, flowers, stars, etc., on the inside of a file folder (four pictures on each side). Draw matching colored pictures on tagboard and cut them out. Cover the gameboard and the cutout pictures with clear Con-Tact paper and tape an envelope on the back of the gameboard for holding the cutouts. To play, let the children take turns placing the cutouts on top of the matching colored pictures on the gameboard.

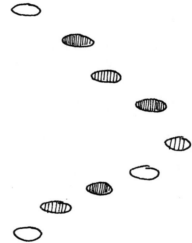

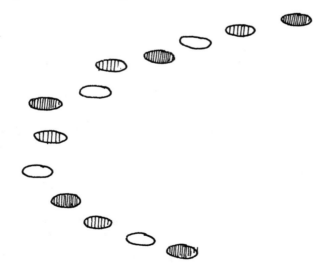

COLORED DOT PATTERNS

On a piece of paper for each child, attach several different colored self-stick dots in a row to start a pattern (red, blue, red, blue; orange, yellow, green, orange, yellow, green; etc.). Then give the children more dots and let them continue the pattern across their papers. When they have finished, start a new pattern on each paper, if desired.

Variation: Make patterns by gluing on circles punched with a hole punch from the desired colors of construction paper.

94

COLOR LOTTO

Make a gameboard by dividing a 9-inch square of tagboard into nine squares and coloring each square a different color. Make game cards by coloring nine 3-inch tagboard squares to match. Tape an envelope on the back of the gameboard for holding the game cards. Then let the children take turns matching the colors by placing the game cards on top of the corresponding colored squares on the gameboard.

COLOR STICKS

Turn a shoebox upside down and cut two parallel rows of slits in the top. Draw different colored dots on the ends of one set of tongue depressors and matching colored dots on the ends of another set. Insert one set of sticks in one of the rows of slits. Then let the children insert matching colored sticks from the second set in the appropriate slits in the other row.

CRAYON COLOR MATCHING

Purchase a box of eight large crayons. On a square of white tagboard, draw an outline of each crayon and fill in the color. Then let the children take turns matching the colors by placing the crayons on top of the corresponding colored shapes on the tagboard square.

COLOR PARKING GARAGE

For this activity you will need a shallow box to use as a parking garage and a number of different colored toy cars. Draw rectangles that match the colors of the cars on the bottom of the box and cut out a doorway in one side. Then let the children "drive" the cars into the garage and "park" them on the matching colored "parking stalls."

COLORED FEATHER GAME

Cut feather shapes out of selected colors of construction paper and place them in a paper bag. Have the children sit in a circle. Let one child at a time reach into the bag and take out a feather. Explain that in order to keep the colored feather, the child must name something that is a matching color (a red apple, a yellow banana, my blue shirt, etc.). Continue the game as long as desired, making sure that everyone ends up with the same number of feathers.

COLOR GRAPH

Conclude your Color Days with a "Rainbow Day" and ask each child to come dressed in his or her favorite color. Make an outline for a bar graph with color names listed down the left-hand side and numerals written across the top. Group the children according to the colors they are wearing and count the number in each group. Then record the results by drawing colored bars on your bar graph outline. Ask questions such as these: "Which group is smaller, the one wearing yellow or the one wearing red? How many more are wearing green than are wearing purple? Which color is the most popular?"

Science

COLORED EYEGLASSES

Make colored eyeglasses for the children to wear on different Color Days. Cut frames out of the desired color of tagboard and glue matching colored cellophane squares over the eyeholes. (Use red, yellow and blue cellophane and combine the colors to make green, orange and purple.) Then attach pipe cleaners to the sides of the frames and bend them to fit over the children's ears.

COLORED CRYSTALS

For each child mix 1 tablespoon Epsom salts and 1 tablespoon water in a baby food jar or a clear plastic glass. Then stir in ¼ teaspoon of the desired color of food coloring. Have the children observe over the next few days as the water evaporates and small crystals begin to form. Keep a magnifying glass on hand for closer examination.

Hint: For the best results, use colors other than yellow.

COLORED ICE CUBES

Tint water with food coloring and freeze to make one tray of red ice cubes, one tray of yellow and one tray of blue. Place three clear plastic glasses on the science table and put a different colored ice cube into each glass. Periodically, have the children observe as the ice changes to colored water. Then place a red ice cube and a yellow ice cube together in another glass and have the children observe as the ice melts and creates orange. Repeat the process using a blue and a yellow ice cube to make green and a red and a blue ice cube to make purple. Then let the children use the remaining colored ice cubes to set up their own color experiments.

SCRATCH 'N SNIFF PAINTS

Add drops of flavoring extract to tempera paints and set them out at an easel. Match the flavors with the paint colors: strawberry or cherry for red, banana or lemon for yellow, peppermint for green, orange for orange, chocolate for brown, anise (licorice) for black, etc. This activity provides a fun sensory experience when working on color recognition and can also be used when studying the sense of smell.

MAKING RAINBOWS

Place a small mirror in a glass of water and tilt it against the side of the glass. Then stand the glass in direct sunlight so that the mirror reflects a rainbow on a wall. Name the rainbow colors with the children (red, orange, yellow, green, blue and purple). Explain that sunlight contains all these colors mixed together, but when it hits the water (or raindrops in the sky), all the colors are separated.

Variation: On a sunny day, use a garden hose to spray a fine mist of water across the sun's rays. Have the children stand with their backs to the sun and look for a rainbow in the mist.

NATURAL DYES

Make dyes by boiling natural ingredients in water. When cool, pour the dyes into small containers. Then let the children take turns dipping small squares of white fabric into the dyes. Try one or more of the following: red onion skins for red, beets for red violet, cranberries for pink, yellow onion skins for yellow, blackberries for blue, spinach leaves for green, coffee for brown.

Variation: Experiment with juices from canned fruits and vegetables such as blueberries, blackberries and beets. Reserve the fruits or vegetables for other uses.

COLOR NATURE WALK

Go on a nature walk with the children to look for various colors. Give them each a small book made of six or more different colored construction paper squares to take with them. Whenever a child spots a nature item that matches the color of a page in his or her book, write the name of the item on the child's page. Then ask the child to look for an item that matches one of the other colored pages. Continue the walk until everyone's book is filled. When you get back, help each child to "read" aloud from his or her color book at circle time.

COLOR MIXING EXPERIMENT

Remove the lids from several Styrofoam egg cartons and fill all the cups with water. Add drops of red, yellow and blue food coloring to several of the cups in each carton. Set out eyedroppers and demonstrate how to use them by "squeezing in" and "letting go." Then let the children use the eyedroppers to experiment with mixing colors by adding drops of the colored water to the cups containing clear water. Encourage them to try creating green, orange, purple and brown and to use the clear water to create lighter shades of the different colors.

Language

COLOR BOOKS

Staple white sheets of construction paper together to make a book for each child. Write "My Color Book" and the child's name on the cover. At the top of each page, glue a different colored construction paper square and write the color name with a matching colored felt-tip marker. Then choose a different color each day and let the children glue matching colored pictures torn or cut from magazines on the appropriate pages in their books.

COLOR PUPPETS

Cut one crayon shape each from the following colors of construction paper: red, yellow, blue, green, orange, purple, brown, black, white. With the points at the top, draw faces on the crayon shapes. Then add construction paper arms and legs and glue each shape on a tongue depressor. Use the color puppets as visual aids when telling color stories or let the children use them for dramatic play.

COLOR BAGS

Use appropriate colored fabric to make a drawstring bag for each Color Day. When you are celebrating Red Day, fill the red bag with small red items (a red button, a red birthday candle, a red building block, etc.). Then at circle time, let each child in turn take an object from the bag and use it for show and tell. Repeat the activity on other Color Days.

COLOR STORY

Make up a story that contains a number of different color words. As you tell the story, have the children raise their hands each time they hear the name of a color.

Variation: Each time you come to a color word in the story, place a colored shape on the flannelboard and have the children name the color.

COLOR WORD PUZZLES

Choose a color such as blue and cut a large crayon shape out of blue tagboard. Divide the shape into four sections and use a felt-tip marker to write each letter of the word "blue" in a section. Cut apart the sections so that they fit together differently. Follow the same procedure to make puzzles for other color words. Then let the children sound out the color words as they piece the puzzles together.

Variation: Make the puzzles out of white tagboard rectangles and write the letters of each color word with a matching colored felt-tip marker.

FLANNELBOARD FUN

Choose a color such as yellow and cut a bird shape out of yellow felt. Place the bird on the flannelboard and recite the poem below. Then ask each child in turn to make up a "little yellow dream" and tell about it. Repeat the activity on other Color Days using different colored birds.

Yellow bird, yellow bird in a tree,
Will you sing a song for me?
If you sing me a song,
Then I'll have a dream.
Yes, I'll have a little yellow dream.

Cindy Dingwall
Palatine, IL

MY GRANDMOTHER'S TRUNK

Play this favorite game on any Color Day. Sit with the children in a circle. If you are celebrating Green Day, spend some time talking about things that are green. Then start the game by saying, "My grandmother went on a trip, and in her trunk she packed a green pickle." Have the child on your right say, "My grandmother went on a trip, and in her trunk she packed a green pickle and a green (leaf/apple/crayon/etc.)." Continue, having each child in turn repeat the list and add another green item to it. Accept any items that could be green (a green ball, a green shirt, etc.) and let the other children help if anyone has trouble remembering the growing list of items.

Hint: When playing the game with younger children, let them each name a colored item without repeating what was said before.

COLOR ROUNDUP

Use this activity on any Color Day to reinforce color recognition and develop language skills. If you are working on blue, assemble as many blue objects as there are children in your group. Place the objects on a tray and have the children sit around it in a circle. Then let each child in turn choose an object, name the color and tell a few sentences about it.

Movement

COLORED MITTEN GAME

Play this game on any Color Day. Cut a mitten shape out of the desired color of construction paper. Have the children sit in a circle with their hands behind their backs and their eyes closed. Walk around the circle and place the mitten shape in one of the children's hands. When you get back to your place, have the children open their eyes while keeping their hands behind their backs. Then sing the song below to the tune of "The Muffin Man" and have the child who is holding the mitten shape respond to the direction. Repeat the game until everyone has had a turn.

> Oh, do you have the (red/blue/etc.) mitten,
> The (red/blue/etc.) mitten,
> The (red/blue/etc.) mitten?
> If you have the (red/blue/etc.) mitten,
> Please (wave it in the air/place it on your knee/etc.).

Joyce Marshall
Whitby, Ontario

RHYTHM STREAMERS

Tape a selected color of crepe paper streamers to the ends of wooden dowels or paper towel tubes. Then let the children wave the streamers as you play music. Vary the tempo to invite slow, flowing movements as well as fast, bouncy ones.

Variation: Tie different colored streamers on the children's wrists and let them dance to music. Periodically, call out directions such as, "Reds, twirl around," or "Blues, wave your streamers high."

MAGIC CARPET

Select a color such as green and place a green carpet square on the floor. Have the children form a line and choose one child to be the leader. Play music and let the children march around the room, crossing over the "magic carpet" as they march. When you stop the music, have the child standing on the carpet name the color. Then let that child be the new leader. Continue the game until everyone has had a turn leading the line.

Variation: Place a number of different colored carpet squares on the floor. When you stop the music, have each child who is standing on a square name the color. Then choose one of those children to be the new leader.

COLORED SQUARES GAME

Cut large squares out of selected colors of construction paper and spread them out on the floor. Then ask the children to perform different actions by giving directions such as these: "Jason, can you put your foot on a red square? Mary, can you hop to a green square? Brian, can you jump over a purple square?" Finally, ask everyone to find a square to stand on and let each child name the color of his or her square.

COLOR PARTNERS

Cut small matching squares out of different colors of construction paper. Place the squares in a paper bag and have each child draw out a square. Play music and let the children move around the room to find their "color partners" by matching up their colored squares. Then have them hold hands with their partners and circle around the room. After everyone has joined the circle, stop the music, collect the colored squares and start the game again.

COLORED FLASHLIGHT DANCING

Unscrew the heads of flashlights and place pieces of colored cellophane under the glass. Turn off the room lights. Then let the children switch on their flashlights and move them to music, making the colored light beams "dance" across the walls, ceiling and floor. Continue the game as long as interest lasts.

Variation: Instead of using cellophane, color the glass of the flashlights with felt-tip markers.

COLORED BEANBAG GAME

Make or purchase beanbags in assorted colors. Have the children sit in a circle and hand out the beanbags. Then play music and let the children pass the beanbags around the circle. Whenever you stop the music, have each child who is holding a beanbag name the color. Continue the game until every child has named at least one color or as long as interest lasts.

Variation: Instead of beanbags, use different colored blocks or squares of tagboard.

TRAFFIC LIGHT GAME

Make a traffic light by covering a half-gallon milk carton with black construction paper and letting the children help glue on red, yellow and green construction paper circles. Discuss what the three colors mean. Then hold up the traffic light and let the children move around the room, pretending to drive cars. When you call out "Green," have them go; when you call out "Yellow," have them slow down; and when you call out "Red," have them stop. Continue the game, letting the children take turns calling out the colors.

Music

COLORED CLOTHES SONG
Sung to: "Frere Jacques"

Children with (red shoes/blue pants/etc.),
Children with (red shoes/blue pants/etc.),
Please stand up, please stand up.
Clap your hands and turn around,
Clap your hands and turn around.
Then sit down, then sit down.

Betty Silkunas
Philadelphia, PA

MARY WORE HER RED DRESS
Sung to: "Did You Ever See a Lassie?"

Mary wore her red dress,
Her red dress, her red dress.
Oh, Mary wore her red dress
To school today.
Her red dress, her red dress,
Her red dress, her red dress.
Oh, Mary wore her red dress
To school today.

Sing a verse for each child, naming a colored item of
clothing that he or she is wearing.

Traditional

DRESSING SONG
Sung to: "The Farmer in the Dell"

I'm putting my (red shirt/blue socks/etc.) on,
I'm putting my (red shirt/blue socks/etc.) on.
I'm getting all dressed to look my best.
I'm putting my (red shirt/blue socks/etc.) on.

Have the children act out dressing movements as they sing
the song.

Elizabeth McKinnon

WEARING COLORS
Sung to: "The Farmer in the Dell"

Oh, David is wearing (red/blue/etc.),
Oh, David is wearing (red/blue/etc.).
Heigh-ho the derry-oh,
David is wearing (red/blue/etc.).

Substitute one of the children's names for "David" each
time you sing the song.

Diana Nazaruk
Clark Lake, MI

IF YOUR CLOTHES HAVE ANY RED

Sung to: "If You're Happy and You Know It"

If your clothes have any red, any red,
If your clothes have any red, any red,
If your clothes have any red,
Put your finger on your head,
If your clothes have any red, any red.

If your clothes have any blue, any blue,
If your clothes have any blue, any blue,
If your clothes have any blue,
Put your finger on your shoe,
If your clothes have any blue, any blue.

If your clothes have any green, any green,
If your clothes have any green, any green,
If your clothes have any green,
Wave your hand so you are seen,
If your clothes have any green, any green.

If your clothes have any yellow, any yellow,
If your clothes have any yellow, any yellow,
If your clothes have any yellow,
Smile like a happy fellow,
If your clothes have any yellow, any yellow.

If your clothes have any brown, any brown,
If your clothes have any brown, any brown,
If your clothes have any brown,
Turn your smile into a frown,
If your clothes have any brown, any brown.

Additional verses: "If your clothes have any black, put your
hands behind your back; If your clothes have any white,
stamp your feet with all your might."

Jean Warren

JOHNNY'S COMING TO SCHOOL

Sung to: "She'll Be Coming Round the Mountain"

Johnny's coming to school today, yes he is.
Johnny's coming to school today, yes he is.
Johnny's coming to school today,
Yes, he's coming to school today,
Yes, he's coming to school today, yes he is.

He'll be dressed all in (red/blue/etc.) when he comes.
He'll be dressed all in (red/blue/etc.) when he comes.
He'll be dressed all in (red/blue/etc.),
He'll be dressed all in (red/blue/etc.),
He'll be dressed all in (red/blue/etc.) when he comes.

Additional verse: "He'll be riding in a (red car/blue truck/etc.)
when he comes." Substitute one of the children's names for
"Johnny" each time you sing the song.

Jean Warren

COLORED SHOES SONG
Sung to: "Looby Loo"

Chorus:
Here we go looby loo,
Here we go looby light.
Here we go looby loo,
All on a Saturday night.

Children with red shoes in,
Children with red shoes out.
Children with red shoes
Shake, shake, shake
And turn yourselves about.

Chorus

Children with blue shoes in,
Children with blue shoes out.
Children with blue shoes
Shake, shake, shake
And turn yourselves about.

Chorus

Continue with additional verses, each time naming a
different shoe color. Have the children stand in a circle
and clap their hands while singing.

Betty Silkunas
Philadelphia, PA

THIS OLD MAN
Sung to: "This Old Man"

This old man, dressed in red,
Wore a red hat on his head.

Chorus:
With a nick nack paddy wack,
Give a dog a bone.
This old man came rolling home.

This old man, dressed in blue,
Tied a blue lace on his shoe.

Chorus

This old man dressed in yellow,
Slept upon a yellow pillow.

Chorus

Jean Warren

PUT YOUR SHAPE IN THE AIR
Sung to: "Twinkle, Twinkle, Little Star"

(First four measures only)

Put your (red/blue/etc.) shape
In the air.
Hold it high
And leave it there.

Put your (red/blue/etc.) shape
On your back.
Now please lay it
On your lap.

Hold your (red/blue/etc.) shape
In your hand.
Now will everyone
Please stand.

Wave your (red/blue/etc.) shape
At the door.
Now please lay it
On the floor.

Hold your (red/blue/etc.) shape
And jump, jump, jump.
Throw your (red/blue/etc.) shape
Way, way up.

Give each child a shape cut from the desired color of
construction paper before singing the song.

Trish Peckham
Raleigh, NC

IN THE BASKET
Sung to: "Ten Little Indians"

Pick up a (red/blue) shape,
Put it in the basket.
Pick up a (red/blue) shape,
Put it in the basket.
Pick up a (red/blue) shape,
Put it in the basket.
Let's count the (red/blue) shapes now.

(Count shapes.)

Place a basket on the floor and lay out shapes cut from the
desired colors of construction paper. Then sing a verse of
the song for each color.

Jean L. Woods
Tulsa, OK

RED SHAPES HOKEY-POKEY
Sung to: "Hokey-Pokey"

Put a red (circle/square/etc.) in,
Put a red (circle/square/etc.) out,
Put a red (circle/square/etc.) in
And shake it all about.
Do the hokey-pokey
And turn yourself around—
That's what it's all about.

Cut different geometric shapes from red construction paper
for the children to use while singing the song. Repeat for
other colors.

Marjorie Debowy
Stony Brook, NY

COLOR DAY SONG
Sung to: "Mary Had a Little Lamb"

Today is our Red Day,
Red Day, Red Day.
Today is our Red Day,
Let's all sing a song.

It will be a fun day,
Fun day, fun day.
It will be a fun day,
Fun day all day long.

Sing a song of Red Day,
Red Day, Red Day.
Sing a song of Red Day,
Sing it all day long.

Substitute other color words for "red" on different Color Days.

Jean Warren

COLOR THUMBKIN
Sung to: "Frere Jacques"

Where is Red Man, where is Red Man?
  (Hold hand in fist.)
Here I am, here I am.
  (Hold up red finger.)
How are you today, sir?
Very well, I thank you.
  (Bend finger up and down.)
Run away, run away.
  (Put finger behind back.)

Tie different colors of yarn (or use colored tape) on the fingers of each child's hand: thumb-red, index finger-blue, middle finger-yellow, ring finger-green, little finger-orange. Then sing a verse of the song for each color.

Betty Silkunas
Philadelphia, PA

VALENTINE COLOR SONG
Sung to: "Twinkle, Twinkle, Little Star"

Valentines red, valentines blue,
Valentines pink say I love you.
Valentines yellow, valentines green,
Prettiest valentines I've ever seen.
Valentines red, valentines blue,
Valentines pink say I love you.

Jean Warren

TEN LITTLE ORANGES
Sung to: "Ten Little Indians"

One little, two little, three little oranges,
Four little, five little, six little oranges,
Seven little, eight little, nine little oranges,
Ten little oranges for me.

Additional verses: "Ten little apples; Ten little lemons; Ten little blueberries; Ten little pickles; Ten little grapes."

Kim Heckert
Adrian, MI

THE REDS CAN TWIRL AROUND
Sung to: "The Farmer in the Dell"

The reds can twirl around,
The reds can twirl around.
Heigh-ho the derry-oh,
The reds can twirl around.

The blues can stamp their feet,
The blues can stamp their feet.
Heigh-ho the derry-oh,
The blues can stamp their feet.

The yellows can touch their toes,
The yellows can touch their toes.
Heigh-ho the derry-oh,
The yellows can touch their toes.

Additional verses: "The greens can clap their hands; The oranges can reach up high; The purples can crouch down low"; etc. Tie colored yarn around the children's wrists before singing the song.

Jean Warren

COLORED BALLOONS
Sung to: "Frere Jacques"

(Red/blue/etc.) balloons,
(Red/blue/etc.) balloons,
Floating up, floating up.
Never let them touch the ground,
Never let them touch the ground.
Keep them up, keep them up.

Let the children pretend to bat balloons up into the air while singing (or use real balloons).

Joyce Marshall
Whitby, Ontario

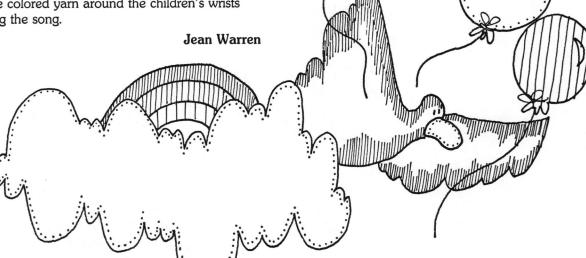

COLORED WAGON SONG
Sung to: "Ten Little Indians"

Hop aboard my little (red/blue/etc.) wagon,
Hop aboard my little (red/blue/etc.) wagon,
Hop aboard my little (red/blue/etc.) wagon.
Let's ride around the room.

'Round and around and around we go,
'Round and around and around we go,
'Round and around and around we go,
All around the room.

Jean Warren

OH, RAINBOW
Sung to: "Oh, Christmas Tree"

Oh, rainbow, oh, rainbow,
How lovely are your colors.
Oh, rainbow, oh, rainbow,
How lovely are your colors.
Purple, red and orange, too,
Yellow, green and blue so true.
Oh, rainbow, oh, rainbow,
How lovely are your colors.

Stella Waldron
Lincoln, NE

Snacks

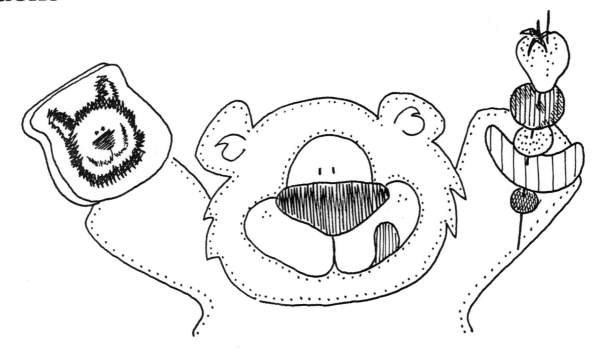

NINE-COLOR FRUIT SALAD

Let the children help prepare a colorful fruit salad using the following fruits: red apple slices (unpeeled), yellow pineapple bits, fresh or frozen blueberries, green honeydew melon chunks, orange segments, purple grapes and "black" raisins. Stir in white mayonnaise. Then mound on paper plates and sprinkle with brown chopped walnuts.

SOUP OF MANY COLORS

Make a pot of chicken or beef broth using bouillon cubes or instant broth mix and water. Then let the children help wash and prepare different colored vegetables to add to the broth. Some suggestions would be red tomatoes, yellow squash, green celery, orange carrots, purple cabbage, brown potatoes (unpeeled), and white onions. Bring the soup to a boil, flavor as desired, then simmer until the vegetables are tender. Let soup cool a bit before serving.

PAINTED BREAD

Set out small bowls of milk and add drops of different colored food coloring to each bowl. Give each of the children a new paint brush (or use Q-Tips) and a slice of white bread. Then let them use the colored milk to paint faces, numbers, flowers, monsters or their own designs on both sides of their bread slices. Toast the bread, spread on melted butter and let the children enjoy their colorful creations.

RAINBOW KEBOBS

For each child thread a strawberry, an orange segment, a pineapple chunk, a honeydew melon ball (or a green grape), a blueberry and a purple grape on a bamboo skewer (or use toothpicks to fasten the fruits together in a row). Serve on top of a lettuce leaf placed on a paper plate along with a small cup of vanilla yogurt to use as a dip. Talk with the children about the rainbow colors of the fruits. Then have them remove the fruits from the skewers before eating their colorful snacks.

Ideas in this chapter were contributed by:

Betty Ruth Baker, Waco, TX
Valerie Bielsker, Lenexa, KS
Vicki Claybrook, Kennewick, WA
Tamara Clohessy, Weaverville, CA
Judy Coiner, West Plains, MO
Marjorie Debowy, Stony Brook, NY
Jeanette Flagge, Fort Dodge, IA
Lena Goehring, Columbus, PA
Jan Goldstein, Indianapolis, IN
Cathy Griffin, Princeton Junction, NJ
Peggy Hanley, St. Joseph, MI
Kim Heckert, Adrian, MI
Colraine Pettipaw Hunley, Doylestown, PA
Ellen Javernick, Loveland, CO
Margery A. Kranyik, Hyde Park, MA
Elizabeth A. Lokensgard, Appleton, WI
Joyce Marshall, Whitby, Ontario

Judith E. McNitt, Adrian, MI
Joleen Meier, Marietta, GA
Susan A. Miller, Kutztown, PA
Inge Mix, Massapequa, NY
Kathy Monahan, Coon Rapids, MN
Cathy Moss, Shavertown, PA
Donna Mullenix, Thousand Oaks, CA
Susan M. Paprocki, Northbrook, IL
Dawn Picollelli, Wilmington, DE
Barbara Robinson, Glendale, AZ
Deborah A. Roessel, Flemington, NJ
Kay Roozen, Des Moines, IA
Betty Silkunas, Philadelphia, PA
Rosemary Spatafora, Pleasant Ridge, MI
JoAnn Yamada, Port Hueneme, CA
Cookie Zingarelli, Columbus, OH

COLOR STORIES, SONGS AND RHYMES
With Flannelboard Patterns

Carl the Clown

By Susan M. Paprocki, Northbrook, IL

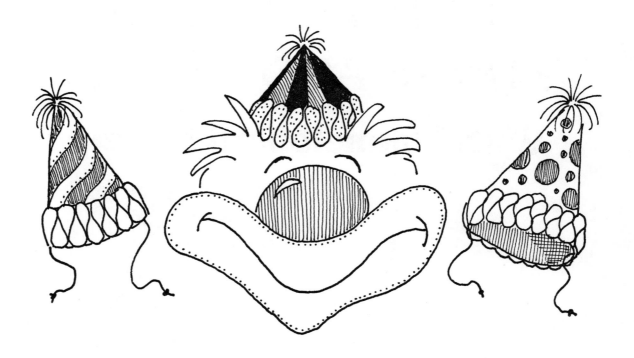

My name, boys and girls, is Carl the Clown.
I wear my hats all over town.

Each one has its own color name,
Which you can learn if you play my game.

Oh, here's a hat, and it is red.
It fits so nicely on my head.

Now when I wear my hat of yellow,
I'm told I'm quite a dandy fellow.

I hope you like my hat of blue.
I'll put in on now, just for you.

My purple hat is just for good.
I'd wear it always if I could.

I wear a white hat on a sunny day.
It looks quite nice, my friends all say.

I put on my green hat to visit the park,
But I take it off when it gets dark.

And when it's dark, I put on brown.
This hat is for a sleepy clown.

Orange and black is for Halloween night.
Yes, indeed, I'm quite a sight!

Preparation: Cut a clown face out of white felt and use felt scraps or felt-tip markers to make hair and facial features. Then cut one clown hat shape each from the following colors of felt: red, yellow, blue, purple, white, green, brown. Cut an additional hat shape out of orange felt and add black decorations.

Activity: Place the clown face on the flannel-board. As you recite the poem, put the appropriate colored hats on the clown's head. When the children have become familiar with the poem, let them take turns placing the hats on the clown's head themselves.

Color Cats

By Susan M. Paprocki, Northbrook, IL

When the cat that is red
Is finally fed,
He raises his head
And says — "Mee-ow!"

When the cat that is blue
Has nothing to do,
He comes up, too,
And whispers — "Mee-ow!"

When the cat that is yellow
Is feeling mellow,
He tends to stretch
And bellow — "Mee-ow!"

When the cat that is brown
Starts stalking the town,
You'll hear his sound
When he cries — "Mee-ow!"

When the cat that is green
Is finally seen,
You'll know what I mean
When I say he can really — "Mee-ow!"

When the cat that is black
Arches his back,
He has an uncanny knack
Of screeching — "Mee-ow!"

When the cat that is white
Comes into your sight,
You very well might
Hear his famous — "Mee-ow!"

Okay, little cats,
Let's hear some "Mee-ows!"
And now it's time
For curtsies and bows.

Preparation: Cut seven cat shapes out of felt, one each from red, blue, yellow, brown, green, black and white.

Activity: As you recite each verse of the poem, place the appropriate colored cat shape on the flannelboard. Encourage the children to try out different kinds of "Mee-ows" for each color cat.

Ha, Ha, Turkey in the Straw

By Jean Warren

Sung to: "Skip to My Lou"

Turkey in the brown straw, ha, ha, ha,
Turkey in the brown straw, ha, ha, ha,
Turkey in the brown straw, ha, ha, ha.
Turkey in the straw, my darling.

Turkey in the white snow, ho, ho, ho,
Turkey in the white snow, ho, ho, ho,
Turkey in the white snow, ho, ho, ho.
Turkey in the snow, my darling.

Turkey in the blue sky, hi, hi, hi,
Turkey in the blue sky, hi, hi, hi,
Turkey in the blue sky, hi, hi, hi.
Turkey in the sky, my darling.

Turkey in the red barn, harn, harn, harn,
Turkey in the red barn, harn, harn, harn,
Turkey in the red barn, harn, harn, harn.
Turkey in the barn, my darling.

Turkey in the yellow corn, horn, horn, horn,
Turkey in the yellow corn, horn, horn, horn,
Turkey in the yellow corn, horn, horn, horn.
Turkey in the corn, my darling.

Turkey in the green tree, hee, hee, hee,
Turkey in the green tree, hee, hee, hee,
Turkey in the green tree, hee, hee, hee.
Turkey in the tree, my darling.

Preparation: Cut a turkey shape out of brown felt and decorate it as desired. Then cut the following shapes out of colored felt for the turkey to "sit" in: a pile of brown straw, a pile of white snow, a blue sky background, a red barn, a yellow bag of corn, a green tree.

Activity: Place all the felt shapes, except for the turkey, on the flannelboard. Then sing the song with the children and let them take turns placing the turkey on the appropriate shapes.

corn

Five Christmas Cookies

By Jean Warren

Five little Christmas cookies,
With frosting galore.
Mother ate the white one,
And then there were four.

Four little Christmas cookies,
Two and two, you see.
Father ate the green one,
And then there were three.

Three little Christmas cookies,
But before I knew,
Sister ate the yellow one,
And then there were two.

Two little Christmas cookies,
Oh, what fun.
Brother ate the brown one,
And then there was one.

One little Christmas cookie,
Watch me run.
I ate the red one,
And then there were none.

Preparation: Cut five Christmas cookie shapes out of felt, one each from white, green, yellow, brown and red.

Activity: Place the cookie shapes on the flannelboard. As you recite the poem, let the children take turns removing the appropriate colored cookies.

121

The Snowman

By Jean Warren

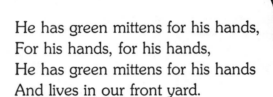

Sung to: "The Muffin Man"

Have you seen the snowman,
The snowman, the snowman,
Have you seen the snowman
Who lives in our front yard?

He has two brown potato eyes,
Potato eyes, potato eyes,
He has two brown potato eyes
And lives in our front yard.

He has an orange carrot nose,
Carrot nose, carrot nose,
He has an orange carrot nose
And lives in our front yard.

He has a bright red berry smile,
Berry smile, berry smile,
He has a bright red berry smile
And lives in our front yard.

He has a big black top hat,
Top hat, top hat,
He has a big black top hat
And lives in our front yard.

He has a long blue woolen scarf,
Woolen scarf, woolen scarf,
He has a long blue woolen scarf
And lives in our front yard.

He has two yellow broomstick arms,
Broomstick arms, broomstick arms,
He has two yellow broomstick arms
And lives in our front yard.

He has green mittens for his hands,
For his hands, for his hands,
He has green mittens for his hands
And lives in our front yard.

He has a big wide purple belt,
Purple belt, purple belt,
He has a big wide purple belt
And lives in our front yard.

Have you seen the snowman,
The snowman, the snowman,
Have you seen the snowman
Who lives in our front yard?

Preparation: Cut a large snowman shape out of white felt. Use other colors of felt to make two brown circles for the snowman's potato eyes, an orange triangle for his carrot nose, small red circles for his berry mouth, a black top hat shape to place on his head, a long blue scarf shape to place at his neck, two yellow broomstick shapes for his arms, two green mitten shapes for his hands and a wide purple belt shape to place at his waist.

Activity: Place the snowman shape on the flannelboard. As you sing the song, put the other shapes on the snowman and watch him come to life. When the children have become familiar with the song, let them take turns placing the shapes on the snowman themselves.

122

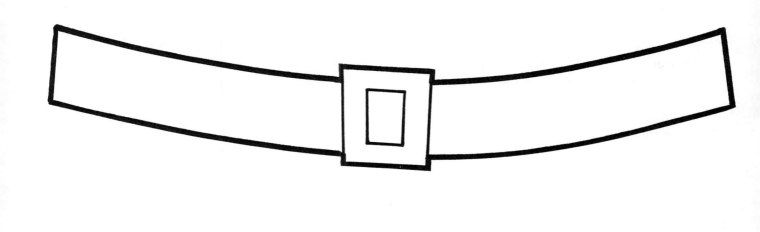

My Kitten's Mitten

By Jean Warren

My poor little kitten lost her mitten
And started to cry, "Boo-hoo."
So I helped my kitten to look for her mitten,
Her beautiful mitten of blue.

I found a mitten just right for a kitten
Under my mother's bed.
But, alas, the mitten was not the right mitten,
For it was colored red.

I found a mitten just right for a kitten
Under my father's pillow.
But, alas, the mitten was not the right mitten,
For it was colored yellow.

I found a mitten just right for a kitten
On the hand of my brother's toy clown.
But, alas, the mitten was not the right mitten,
For it was colored brown.

I found a mitten just right for a kitten
Under the laundry so clean.
But, alas, the mitten was not the right mitten,
For it was colored green.

I found a mitten just right for a kitten
Inside a grocery sack.
But, alas, the mitten was not the right mitten,
For it was colored black.

I found a mitten just right for a kitten
Under the kitchen sink.
But, alas, the mitten was not the right mitten,
For it was colored pink.

I found a mitten just right for a kitten
Inside my favorite shoe.
And this time the mitten was just the right mitten,
For it was colored blue!

Preparation: Cut a kitten shape out of white felt. Then cut two mitten shapes out of blue felt and one mitten shape each out of red, yellow, brown, green, black and pink.

Activity: Place the kitten shape on the flannelboard and put a blue mitten shape on one of its paws. As you recite the poem, place the appropriate colored mittens, one at a time, on the kitten's other paw. When the children become familiar with the poem, leave off the last word in each verse and let them supply the rhyming color word.

When March Hats Blow

By Jean Warren

When I hear the March winds blow,
I look up in the sky.
Instead of things like birds or planes,
I watch the hats fly by.

Each one different from the last,
Every color do I see.
Some are big and some are small,
As they fly by me.

Here comes a blue hat flying by,
Now a yellow hat in the sky.
Next a red hat on its way,
Then a brown hat flies away.

Green and black, orange and white,
Even purple—what a sight!
I like it when there's rain and snow,
But most of all when March hats blow.

Preparation: Cut nine different hat shapes out of felt, one each from blue, yellow, red, brown, green, black, orange, white and purple.

Activity: Place the hat shapes on the left side of the flannelboard. As you recite the poem, "fly" the appropriate colored hats across the flannelboard to the right side. Then repeat the poem and let the children help decide the order of the colors (except for white).

Four Easter Eggs

By Jean Warren

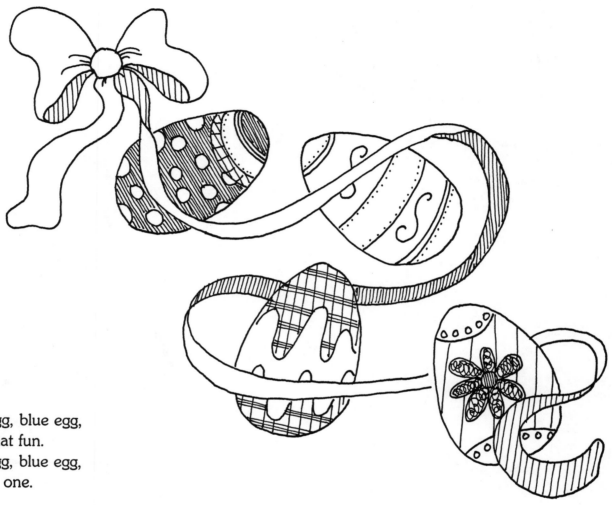

Blue egg, blue egg,
Oh, what fun.
Blue egg, blue egg,
I found one.

Green egg, green egg,
I see you.
Green egg, green egg,
Now I've two.

Red egg, red egg,
Can you see?
Red egg, red egg,
Now I've three.

Yellow egg, yellow egg,
Just one more.
Yellow egg, yellow egg,
Now I've four.

Preparation: Cut four egg shapes out of felt, one each from blue, green, red and yellow.

Activity: Recite the poem with the children and let them take turns placing the appropriate colored egg shapes on the flannelboard. Repeat the poem until every child has had at least one turn.

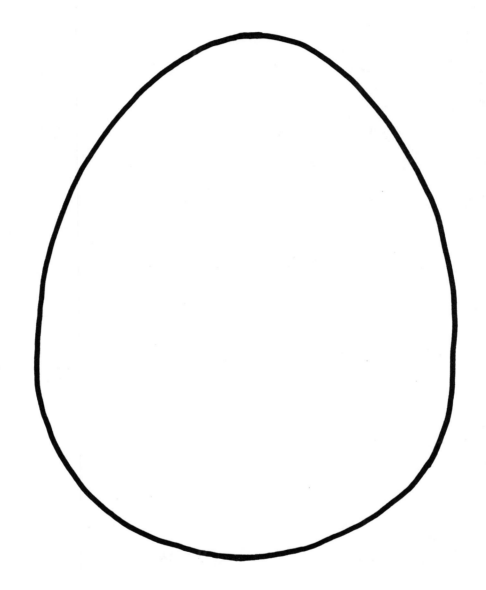

Hunting for Eggs

By Jean Warren

Hunting for eggs,
Under my bed,
I found one in a slipper,
And the egg was colored red.

Hunting for eggs,
Now I have two,
I found one in the closet,
And the egg was colored blue.

Hunting for eggs,
What a lucky fellow,
I found one in a bucket,
And the egg was colored yellow.

Hunting for eggs,
Where none could be seen,
I found one in a shoebox,
And the egg was colored green.

Hunting for eggs,
Quick as a wink,
I found one in the garden,
And it was colored pink.

Red and yellow,
Green, pink and blue.
I found five eggs—
How about you?

Preparation: Cut one egg shape each from the following colors of felt: red, blue, yellow, green, pink. Cut an Easter basket shape out of any other color of felt.

Activity: Place the Easter basket shape on the flannelboard and read aloud the first five verses of the poem. When you come to the last line of each verse, place the appropriate colored egg shape in the basket and let the children name the color word. Then read the last verse and have the children point to the eggs as you name the colors.

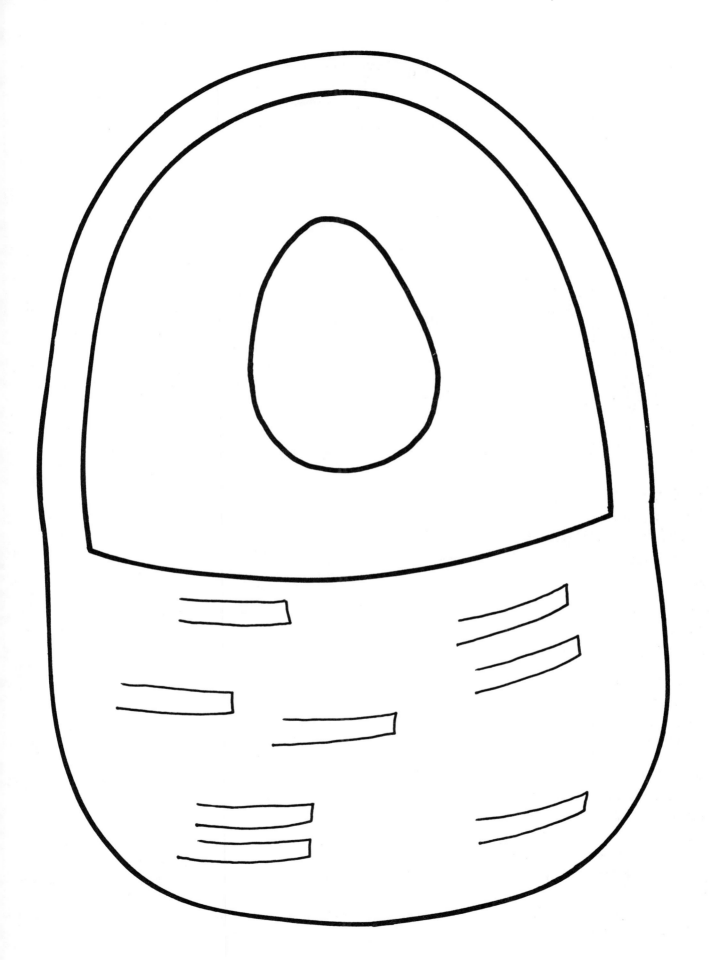

Springtime

Adapted From a Story by
Mildred Hoffman, Tacoma, WA

This is the yellow sun up in the sky.
This is a bluebird flying by.

This is the green grass under my feet.
These are red flowers that smell so sweet.

This is a brown tree that grows straight and tall.
These are pink blossoms just starting to fall.

And this is an orange caterpillar, so soon to be
A white butterfly for the spring world to see!

Preparation: Cut the following shapes out of felt:
a yellow sun, a blue bird, a strip of green grass,
two or more red flowers, a brown tree, several
pink blossoms, an orange caterpillar, a white
butterfly.

Activity: As you recite the poem, place the
appropriate felt shapes on the flannelboard to
create a colorful spring scene. When the children
have become familiar with the poem, let them
take turns placing the shapes on the flannelboard
themselves.

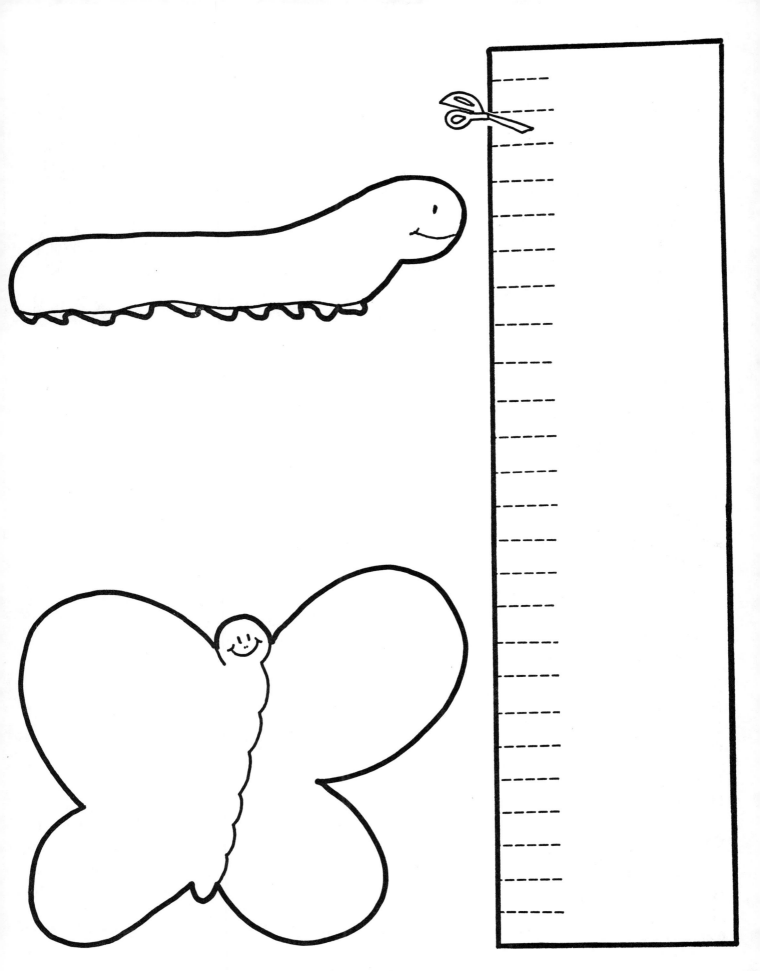

141

Color Birds

By Jean Warren

Yellow bird, yellow bird,
High in a tree,
How many yellow things
Can you see?

Blue bird, blue bird,
High in a tree,
How many blue things
Can you see?

Red bird, red bird,
High in a tree,
How many red things
Can you see?

Black bird, black bird,
High in a tree,
How many black things
Can you see?

Green bird, green bird,
High in a tree,
How many green things
Can you see?

White bird, white bird,
High in a tree,
How many white things
Can you see?

Orange bird, orange bird,
High in a tree,
How many orange things
Can you see?

Purple bird, purple bird,
High in a tree,
How many purple things
Can you see?

Brown bird, brown bird,
High in a tree,
How many brown things
Can you see?

Preparation: Cut one bird shape each from the following colors of felt: yellow, blue, red, black, green, white, orange, purple, brown.

Activity: As you recite each verse of the poem, place the appropriate colored bird shape on the flannelboard. Then ask the children to name things they can see around them that are the same color.

Color Balloons

By Jean Warren

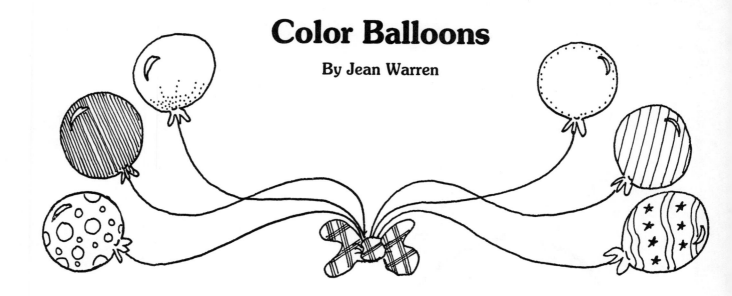

I had a great big red balloon,
Until I let it go.
Now where, oh where, I wonder,
Did my balloon blow?

I had a great big blue balloon,
The string I held so tight.
But when I opened up my hand,
My balloon flew out of sight.

I had a great big green balloon,
As pretty as could be.
But when I let go of its string,
It flew away from me.

I had a great big yellow balloon,
When I went out to play.
But when I wasn't watching,
My balloon just flew away.

Red balloon, red balloon,
Where can you be?
Red balloon, red balloon,
Up in a tree.

Blue balloon, blue balloon,
Where did you fly?
Blue balloon, blue balloon,
Up in the sky.

Green balloon, green balloon,
Where can you be?
Green balloon, green balloon,
Under the tree.

Yellow balloon, yellow balloon,
Where did you fly?
Yellow balloon, yellow balloon,
High in the sky.

Preparation: Cut four balloon shapes out of felt, one each from red, blue, green and yellow. Then use felt to make an outdoor scene on the flannelboard: a blue sky background, a yellow sun in the sky, a tree with several large red apple shapes on it and a strip of tall green grass under the tree. (Make the sun, apple and grass shapes a little bit larger than the balloon shapes.)

Activity: As you recite each of the first four verses of the poem, hold up the appropriate colored balloon. When you come to the last line of each verse, "fly" the balloon to the flannelboard and place it on a matching color (the red balloon on a red apple, the blue balloon on the blue sky, the green balloon on the green grass and the yellow balloon on the yellow sun). As you recite the last four verses of the poem, let the children take turns finding the "hidden" balloons and removing them from the flannelboard.

144

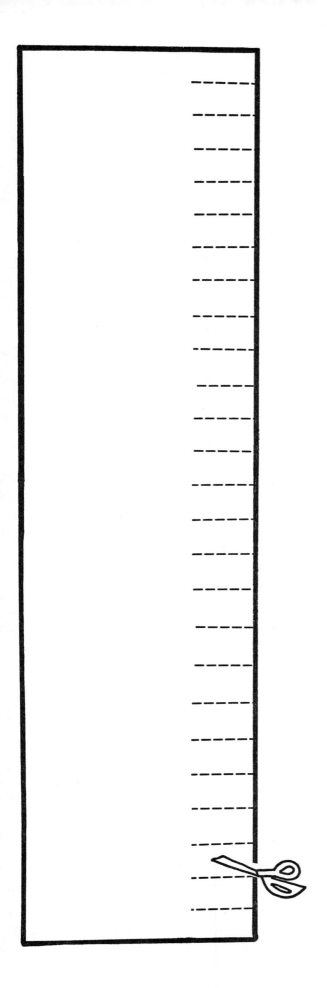

Out in the Garden

By Jean Warren

Sung to: "Down by the Station"

Out in the garden early in the morning,
See the red tomatoes all in a row.
See the happy farmer coming out to pick them.
Pick, pick, pick, pick, off (he/she) goes.

Out in the garden early in the morning,
See the yellow squashes all in a row.
See the happy farmer coming out to pick them.
Pick, pick, pick, pick, off (he/she) goes.

Out in the garden early in the morning,
See the blueberries all in a row.
See the happy farmer coming out to pick them.
Pick, pick, pick, pick, off (he/she) goes.

Out in the garden early in the morning,
See the green string beans all in a row.
See the happy farmer coming out to pick them.
Pick, pick, pick, pick, off (he/she) goes.

Out in the garden early in the morning,
See the orange carrots all in a row.
See the happy farmer coming out to pick them.
Pick, pick, pick, pick, off (he/she) goes.

Out in the garden early in the morning,
See the purple cabbages all in a row.
See the happy farmer coming out to pick them.
Pick, pick, pick, pick, off (he/she) goes.

Preparation: From felt cut out four red tomato shapes, four yellow squash shapes, four blue blueberry shapes, four green string bean shapes, four orange carrot shapes and four purple cabbage shapes.

Activity: Place the shapes on the flannelboard in rows of four (four carrots, four tomatoes, etc.). As you sing the song, let the children take turns being the happy farmer and "picking" the appropriate rows of vegetables or fruits by removing the shapes from the flannelboard.

DANCING COLORS

Dancing Colors

By Jean Warren

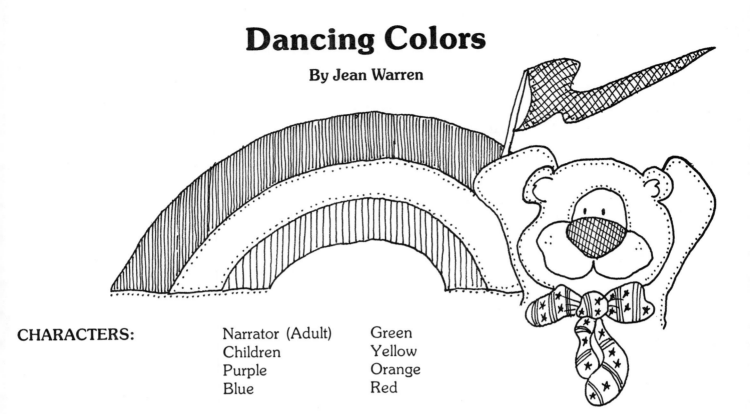

CHARACTERS:

Narrator (Adult)	Green
Children	Yellow
Purple	Orange
Blue	Red

(Children are lined up at back of stage.)

NARRATOR: Look, children! The colors are dancing into town!

(Groups of Purple, Blue, Green, Yellow, Orange and Red dance onstage.)

CHILDREN: **THE COLORS ARE DANCING INTO TOWN**
Sung to: "When Johnny Comes Marching Home"

The colors are dancing into town, hurray, hurray!
The colors are dancing into town, we hope they stay.
The colors dance in, there's purple and blue,
Green, yellow, orange and red, too.
Oh, we're all so glad, we hope they want to stay.

The colors are dancing all around, hurray, hurray!
The colors are dancing all around, we hope they stay.
The colors are dancing here and there,
The colors are dancing everywhere.
Oh, we're all so glad, we hope they want to stay.

The colors are making everything so bright today,
The colors are making everything so bright and gay.
The colors dance in, there's purple and blue,
Green, yellow, orange and red, too.
Oh, we're all so glad, we hope they want to stay.

(Colors dance to back of stage. Purple steps forward and begins dancing and placing purple objects around stage. Other Colors sing along with Children.)

CHILDREN:

PURPLE IS DANCING ALL AROUND
Sung to: "When Johnny Comes Marching Home"

Purple is dancing all around, hurray, hurray!
Purple is dancing all around, we hope it stays.
Eggplants, grapes and violets, too,
Purple, we love you! Yes, we do!
And we're all so glad that purple is here today.

(Purple dances to back of stage. Blue steps forward and begins dancing and placing blue objects around stage. Other Colors sing along with Children.)

CHILDREN:

BLUE IS DANCING ALL AROUND
Sung to: "When Johnny Comes Marching Home"

Blue is dancing all around, hurray, hurray!
Blue is dancing all around, we hope it stays.
Sky and lakes and bluebirds, too,
Blue, we love you! Yes, we do!
And we're all so glad that blue is here today.

(Blue dances to back of stage. Green steps forward and begins dancing and placing green objects around stage. Other Colors sing along with Children.)

CHILDREN:

GREEN IS DANCING ALL AROUND
Sung to: "When Johnny Comes Marching Home"

Green is dancing all around, hurray, hurray!
Green is dancing all around, we hope it stays.
Grass and trees and lettuce, too,
Green, we love you! Yes, we do!
And we're all so glad that green is here today.

(Green dances to back of stage. Yellow steps forward and begins dancing and placing yellow objects around stage. Other Colors sing along with Children.)

CHILDREN:

YELLOW IS DANCING ALL AROUND
Sung to: "When Johnny Comes Marching Home"

Yellow is dancing all around, hurray, hurray!
Yellow is dancing all around, we hope it stays.
Bananas, sun and lemons, too,
Yellow, we love you! Yes, we do!
And we're all so glad that yellow is here today.

(Yellow dances to back of stage. Orange steps forward and begins dancing and placing orange objects around stage. Other Colors sing along with Children.)

CHILDREN:

ORANGE IS DANCING ALL AROUND
Sung to: "When Johnny Comes Marching Home"

Orange is dancing all around, hurray, hurray!
Orange is dancing all around, we hope it stays.
Pumpkins, juice and carrots, too,
Orange, we love you! Yes, we do!
And we're all so glad that orange is here today.

(Orange dances to back of stage. Red steps forward and begins dancing and placing red objects around stage. Other Colors sing along with Children.)

CHILDREN:

RED IS DANCING ALL AROUND
Sung to: "When Johnny Comes Marching Home"

Red is dancing all around, hurray, hurray!
Red is dancing all around, we hope it stays.
Apples, berries, cherries, too,
Red, we love you! Yes, we do!
And we're all so glad that red is here today.

(Other Colors step forward and join Red in dancing around stage.)

CHILDREN:

THE COLORS ARE DANCING ALL AROUND
Sung to: "When Johnny Comes Marching Home"

The colors are dancing all around the town today,
The colors are dancing all around, we hope they stay.
First they're low and then they're high,
Now they're dancing in the sky.
And we're all so glad the colors came to stay.

(Colors line up as if forming a rainbow, with Purple at the "bottom" and Red at the "top.")

NARRATOR: Oh, look! The colors have made a rainbow!

ALL CHARACTERS: **RAINBOW COLORS**
Sung to: "Hush, Little Baby"

Rainbow purple, rainbow blue,
Rainbow green and yellow, too.
Rainbow orange, rainbow red,
Rainbow smiling overhead.

Come and count the colors with me.
How many colors can you see?
One, two, three, up to green,
Four, five, six colors can be seen.

Rainbow purple, rainbow blue,
Rainbow green and yellow, too.
Rainbow orange, rainbow red,
Rainbow smiling overhead.

THE END

Prop and Costume Suggestions

Use any or all of the prop and costume ideas listed below, depending upon how elaborate you want your musical production to be. You can use "Dancing Colors" as an ongoing activity for story time or music time or as a basis for staging a performance in front of an audience.

- Make colored construction paper headbands for the Colors to wear.
- Provide colored objects or paper cutouts for the Colors to place around the stage area.
- Have the Colors dress in the colors they are representing.
- Make a dancing cape for each of the Colors. Tape appropriate colored crepe paper strips to a long piece of yarn. Safety-pin the center of the yarn to the back of the child's collar and tie the ends together in front. (Or tie the yarn around the child's waist, if desired.)
- If you are performing the musical in front of an audience, make a rainbow mural to use as a stage backdrop. Paint colored arcs from top to bottom in this order: red, orange, yellow, green, blue, purple.

Totline® Newsletter

Activities, songs and new ideas to use right now are waiting for you in every issue!

Each issue puts the fun into teaching with 32 pages of challenging and creative activities for young children. Included are open-ended art activities, learning games, music, language and science activities plus 8 reproducible pattern pages.

Published bi-monthly.

Sample issue - $2.00

Super Snack News

Nutritious snack ideas, related songs, rhymes and activities

- Teach young children health and nutrition through fun and creative activities.

- Use as a handout to involve parents in their children's education.

- Promote quality child care in the community with these handouts.

- Includes nutritious sugarless snacks, health tidbits, and developmentally appropriate activities.

- Published monthly.

- Easily reproducible.

With each subscription you are given the right to:

Make up to:
200 COPIES per issue

Sample issue - $2.00

Warren Publishing House, Inc. • P.O. Box 2250, Dept. Z • Everett, WA 98203

Totline® Books

Super Snacks
Teaching Tips
Teaching Toys
Piggyback® Songs
More Piggyback® Songs
Piggyback® Songs for Infants and Toddlers
Piggyback® Songs in Praise of God
Piggyback® Songs in Praise of Jesus
Holiday Piggyback® Songs
Animal Piggyback® Songs
Piggyback® Songs for School

1•2•3 Art
1•2•3 Games
1•2•3 Colors
1•2•3 Puppets
1•2•3 Murals
1•2•3 Books
Teeny-Tiny Folktales
Short-Short Stories
Mini-Mini Musicals
Small World Celebrations
Special Day Celebrations
Yankee Doodle Birthday Celebrations
Great Big Holiday Celebrations
"Cut & Tell" Scissor Stories for Fall
"Cut & Tell" Scissor Stories for Winter
"Cut & Tell" Scissor Stories for Spring
Seasonal Fun
Alphabet Theme-A-Saurus
Theme-A-Saurus
Theme-A-Saurus II
Toddler Theme-A-Saurus
Alphabet & Number Rhymes
Color, Shape & Season Rhymes
Object Rhymes
Animal Rhymes
Our World
"Mix & Match" Animal Patterns
"Mix & Match" Everyday Patterns
"Mix & Match" Holiday Patterns
"Mix & Match" Nature Patterns
ABC Space
ABC Farm
ABC Zoo
ABC Circus

Available at school supply stores and parent/teacher stores or write for our catalog.

Warren Publishing House, Inc. • P.O. Box 2250, Dept. B • Everett, WA 98203